BLURB

In 2005, Jon Shukurov left Uzbekistan for the United States. He was determined to make a better life for himself. He was not prepared for what greeted him in the land of opportunity. A baffling bureaucratic immigration process, slave-like work conditions, and a discouraging blast of culture shock all seemed to be conspiring to send him back home, tail tucked between his legs. Fast forward more than a decade and half later, and he is a successful entrepreneur and contributor to his community and beyond.

How did he manage this?

That's what this book is all about.

If you are planning to immigrate or have just arrived in the United States, daunted by the confusing process of legal immigration and the difficulties of joining an alien society, allow Jon to share his knowledge and experience.

In these pages you will find clear, concise, practical information on:

- Gaining legal status
- Understanding your basic rights
- Accessing available social services
- Obtaining the proper identification

- Overcoming culture shock and dealing with assimilation and cultural maintenance
- Handling your personal finances
- Prioritizing your English-language skills
- Adopting a mindset that will set you up for success
- Starting your own business
- And more!

You may still be on the fence or may have just taken a frightening and incredible first step to remaking your life. Let Jon's book be your companion on this amazing journey as you transition from newcomer to U.S. citizen to productive, successful member of the American community.

THE IMMIGRANT'S COMPANION

Making Your American
Dream a Reality

ASRORJON N. SHUKUROV

ISBN: 979-8-89079-011-8 (Hardcover)
ISBN: 979-8-89079-012-5 (Paperback)
ISBN: 979-8-89079-013-2 (Ebook)

I understand the solitude of navigating this journey alone; nobody should have to endure it solo. This book is your steadfast companion, offering valuable insights at any life stage. Unlike traditional books, you have the freedom to skip chapters and focus on what matters most to you. Upon completion, discover avenues to connect with the author for additional resources, further propelling your pursuit of the American Dream.

TABLE OF CONTENTS

Why I Wrote This Book - When I arrived in the States, everything was new to me: people, language, laws, regulations, ethics, norms, and the list goes on and on. While searching for the answers to overcome my problems, I ended up finding solutions through various resources; some of this took years, if not decades.

This book intends to help fellow immigrants avoid my mistakes and guide them to a better future, while having a smoother ride along the way. It's filled with actionable advice from which you, the reader, can benefit, starting immediately. Although it won't answer every question and problem, it's designed to not only provide a helping hand for specific issues, but also to teach you a process for solving problems more generally.

I recall a sense of feeling lost while trying to navigate this new environment. Most of this was due to my background, my history, and my mentality. This led me to believe that my past and how I thought and processed things were disadvantages. As I ground my way through the American Dream, I started to notice that the things I thought were holding me back were actually advantages propelling me to new heights and pushing/pulling me through the hard times. In addition, my immigrant mentality of putting in countless hours in two to three jobs, looking for opportunities everywhere, and having an entrepreneurial mind have aided me. Now, I know with certainty that my past experiences and my immigrant mentality are strengths and not weaknesses. My hope is, as you go through these pages, you too will realize not only the same but also leverage your strengths to achieve your brighter and better future.

Who This Book Is For - If you feel insecure, helpless, cornered, and/or all alone facing challenges due to immigrating to this country, let this book be your faithful companion throughout your journey. If you feel like you have been in the States for years, yet there is still a lot more you want to accomplish and you don't know where to look for help, let this book be your guide. If you are full of ambitions, hungry for knowledge, and unsure how to get from where you are to where you want to be, let this volume become your daily handbook.

-   Asrorjon Shukurov

HOW DID IT ALL BEGIN?

I was a teenager in the early aughts when I decided to leave Uzbekistan. It was not for lack of love and support. My parents were teachers, and they worked hard to ensure the needs of the family were met; by all accounts, I grew up in an upper-middle-class home. But the Soviet experience still haunted the nation, and despite a loving family, a good education, and economic security, I felt that I was choking on the rules and norms—wear a suit and tie, no drinking, watch what you say, carry ID in case the police have questions—and I wanted to breathe freely. And the winds blowing from the once mysterious and closed-off West were fresh, a little unruly, and scented with wonder, adventure, and opportunity. Rock and roll, the Sony Walkman, and blue jeans.

Of course, for me, the West really meant America—the United States of America.

And of course, such a dream was just that—a dream. An impossibility. But deep in my heart, I believed I would make that dream come true.

In 2005, with $200 in my pocket and a single bag of clothes, I flew in an airplane for the first time in my life. It remains the longest flight I have ever taken. The approach to JFK amazed me. New York City splashed across the land, a galaxy of lights, the perfect herald for the land of magic and wealth.

My only contact was a cousin who I had only spoken to twice before. Although a close friend to my late brother, I had no idea how he would react when I called him. As it turned out, he was a huge source of initial support for me. My plan was simple. I would work in the U.S. for five years, then return to Uzbekistan with enough money to purchase a house and a car and take a managerial job with the Uzbek government, which even now remains more stable than the private sector. It never occurred to me to remain in the US, to build a life there.

But the plunge into an alien environment had a curious effect on me. I experienced true culture shock, and so abrupt was the jolt that it jarred my mindset, which was entrenched in the old Soviet bureaucratic ways, in a sense, setting it free.

My first obstacle was the U.S. immigration system, a cumbersome and complex labyrinth to navigate. To be fair, it's not the worst system in the world, and some countries don't offer any pathway to naturalization, but as I had never any need to expose myself to Uzbekistan's system, it was certainly daunting. However, I prevailed, obtaining an H2B, unqualified work visa, through my first employer, in the hotel industry, which eventually allowed me to get a U.S. visa. That was perhaps the only good thing about my first employer.

Given my prior experience, I was promised work as a receptionist, front desk clerk, or room service wait staff. Instead, I found myself in housekeeping (which would prove prophetic). The employer provided a sparsely furnished trailer where I lived with eleven other souls on the remote outskirts of Denver, Colorado. A single landline phone, outdated TV, and one poorly ventilated bathroom to serve us all. The employer would pick us up in the morning and take us to work. At the end of shift, we'd stop at a grocery store where they would buy us food and sundries. The employer never paid me for my labor. Imagine my humiliation and disillusionment to discover that slavery still existed in the great United States of America.

My cousin helped me escape that toxic environment. He also assisted me with housing, a car, and a new job as a nighttime porter at a supermarket in Baltimore, Maryland. On top of that, I took a morning janitorial shift at Marshall's, an off-price department store (I would eventually become a stocker there). For the next two years I worked seven nights a week, 10 p.m. to 6 a.m., and most mornings. I was exhausted and resorted to various ways to stay awake while driving to Safeway: speak to my parents on the phone, keep the windows open even in freezing winter, smoke, sing real loud, scream.

Eventually, I opted for a valet job at the Admiral Fell Inn in Baltimore, Maryland. I made three dollars an hour, a third of what I could've been making serving banquets, but it paved the way for a position at the front desk where I began to learn computing.

My arrival in Baltimore also marked another change. Until that time, I had no social life. But in Baltimore, away from the awful conditions in Colorado and no longer surrounded solely by my immigrant community, I began to experience American things. I made friends and built relationships that are strong to this day.

I turned down a promotion to supervisor at the hotel and instead accepted a position as office administrator for a construction and development company. It was there that I learned the essential skills I needed to start my own business, which I did in 2009, when I walked away from a secure job and stepped into the unknown, founding Interworld Cleaning, Inc.

After three years working nonstop to build my company, I began to see the fruits of my labor: I took a trip to Puerto Rico, bought a new car, purchased a house, and got married. Everything was coming together, and it hit a crescendo in 2018 when I purchased my first mixed-use property, which is still where my office is located.

But the freedom and opportunity available in the U.S. mean that there are far less imposed guardrails on the decisions you make. That is, the freedom to succeed also means the freedom to fail. In 2019, this was made painfully clear to me when, after a period of time spent caught up in selfish pursuits and losing sight of what was truly important, my wife took our two daughters and left me to return to Uzbekistan.

When people ask me why I came to America, I just say Hollywood. They look at me a little strangely. Then I explain that I came to America not to act but to follow the "American Dream," which is expressed so eloquently in Hollywood movies: the big single-family house, two cars in the garage, a couple of kids and a pet or two frolicking in the large backyard, and, of course, the dollars growing on trees everywhere just waiting to be picked by the bushel.

I learned quickly that Hollywood's American Dream was really just a pipe dream, and that the real American Dream required getting into the trenches, getting dirty, and most importantly, taking risks. A life of guaranteed safety without risks strikes me more as a prison sentence than an actual life where I took personal responsibility, dictated the terms, and lived to my fullest. So I took chances and I faced uncertainty.

You're thinking of coming to America or you're already here. You've got a lot to do just to get settled. I've done it all. I've made my way through the immigration system, social services, the job market, the financial system, and a new culture. All of that is waiting for you, and I've experienced a lot of it, and I've made a lot of mistakes.

My late brother used to say that a smart person learns from his mistakes, but he also said that a wise person learns from other people's mistakes. I want you to become a wise person. I welcome you to learn from my mistakes, take from my experience, and know that you have a companion on this long, strange American trip.

CHAPTER 1

WHY AMERICA: WHAT IS THE AMERICAN DREAM?

For all the internal struggles it may experience, the United States still shines as a beacon of hope and opportunity for millions of people around the globe. They see a land of invention, of opportunity, and of greatness that doesn't discriminate based on social class or background–a place where anyone can show up, not knowing the language and without a cent in their pocket, and still manage to create a better life for themselves and their family. This equality of opportunity is what people all over the world still venerate as the American[1] Dream.

---

[1] Please note that the term "America" and "Americans" in English and in many parts of the world typically refer to the country of the United States of America and the people who live there. This is primarily due to the use of the seven-continent model, in which "The Americas" are two continents, making it clear that the singular "America" does not refer to them. This can cause some misunderstandings, especially in Latin American countries where the six-continent model is most prevalent. In this model, "America" refers to the singular continent, and a separate word even exists in Spanish

In 1776, the Declaration of Independence stated that "all men are created equal" with the rights to "life, liberty, and the pursuit of happiness." These words paved the way for the idea that anyone in America, regardless of their status at birth, could improve their lives and achieve their dreams through hard work and individual capabilities. Through this new ideal, the concept of social mobility arose in which an individual's or family's social status was not permanent and could be changed through effort and will.

Social mobility often occurs between generations where parents or grandparents have spent their lives working to allow their children and grandchildren to have better lives. This intergenerational social mobility is often the goal of immigration to the United States. We immigrants came here with our children or to start families knowing that our children would be better off. We hope that our children will be free from the burden of language barriers or uncertain citizenship status—hopes that are often realized by policies that support and protect immigrant children. Unfortunately, no ideal is perfect. Ultimately, the circumstances of our birth have profound effects on how our lives

---

for people from the United States: *Estadounidense*. Just know that this is primarily a linguistic and regional difference, and any use of "America" in this book in reference to referring to the United States is not meant to exclude other parts of the Americas. Rather, it is just the most commonly accepted term. That said, I try to stick to using "United States" to avoid any ambiguity, especially given the wide audience of this book. The terms Latin America, North America, and South America will be used to refer to other regions of the Americas.

play out. Equality of opportunity has certainly advanced throughout the years: being born a baker's son doesn't mean you too must be a baker for the rest of your days. Being a woman doesn't mean you can't have a successful career or remain independent of male relatives.

However, your background does still impact your opportunities. Being born poor means you must work harder to gain money than those who were born into wealth. Starting your own business from scratch will be more grueling than taking over a family business. And immigrating from another country can have countless setbacks, whether it's the language barrier, effects of violence and poverty from the country of origin, the expenses and time needed for the immigration process, or much much more.

The main takeaway is that it IS possible to change your destiny—and drastically. To say it is impossible is to disregard what sets America apart from other nations. However, it will be hard, and anyone who claims that achieving the American Dream requires the same amount of work for everyone, regardless of their background, is naive. You might have to work a lot harder than other people. You might not be able to climb as far up the ladder. But you can make a better life for yourself and for the generations that follow you, and those generations can continue the pattern, making the world as a whole a better place one small step at a time.

There is no singular American Dream. There is no goal post that you need to reach to say you've achieved it. It is merely the opportunity to improve your life by taking action. Not everyone will be able to become a millionaire or the next president, but that's okay. Happiness and success are different for each person, and no one should base their dreams on what they are told they should achieve. Some people want a simple life with their family and a white picket fence, while others want adventure or success in business. Some simply want to live in peace, free of the threats in their native countries that many Americans can't even imagine. Take the opportunity provided by immigration, make your own goals, and set about achieving them. Create your own dream.

But why create that dream in the United States? Part of the answer is geographic practicality. This is true for anyone leaving a country in Latin America or of low economic means. In most cases, it's easier and cheaper to get here than to travel all the way to somewhere such as Eurasia, Africa, or Australia.

It's also more likely that people will speak your language if you're from Latin America, as Spanish is fairly common in the U.S. But, it's still more than that. The U.S. is really a place of prosperity, where even those who aren't terribly well-off are living at levels well above many people from undeveloped and developing countries. This doesn't mean poverty and harsh conditions don't exist: in fact, a report by the UN in 2018[2] shows that certain parts of the U.S. have levels of extreme poverty as high as those of the world's least-developed countries. But, again, it's not necessarily the current situation that draws immigrants. It's the opportu-

---

[2] "Report of the Special Rapporteur on extreme poverty and human rights on his mission to the United States of America", United Nations National Assembly, accessed 4 Mar. 2022, https://undocs.org/A/HRC/38/33/ADD.1.

nity. It's knowing that the tools for pulling yourself out of poverty exist, and you can take advantage of them.

The country provides practically limitless opportunity to grow if you know how to take advantage of what's available. Many of the greatest and wealthiest people in modern history are from the U.S., known for the changes they make and the innovation they spark. Everyone, even those from isolated villages in developing countries, can name powerful people from the U.S. Whether it's presidents, entrepreneurs, celebrities, scientists, we all know some names. And nearly all of these people either are—or are descended from—immigrants. This is a unique aspect of the makeup of the U.S. It was founded by immigrants, and has continually taken in more throughout its history. Not many places can claim a background that has depended so heavily on immigrants, and benefited so greatly from them.

Congratulations on finishing Chapter 1!

Use the following questions to help you reflect on the chapter you just read.

1. What is your motivation - your WHY - for wanting to immigrate to the U.S.?

2. What advantages and benefits are you looking forward to?

3. What are the top 3 States you would like to live in?

Your progress so far   8%

1/13

CHAPTER 2

HOW TO IMMIGRATE TO THE U.S.

LEGAL IMMIGRATION

In this chapter, we will primarily focus on the legal aspect of immigration, such as the most common visa types, application process, ways to enter the United States, how to petition for your loved ones, permanent resident (Green Card), and eventually, the naturalization process.

At the very end of this chapter, I will shed some light on the rights and responsibilities of undocumented aliens and the possible path to their legalization.

Immigrating legally to the U.S. is the best path to take and can benefit you and the country. This might be easier said than done, especially given that some policies and government functions make undocumented immigration easier than legal immigration, depending on the situation. Although the pathway might be complex, the benefits far outweigh those that might accrue through illegal immigration.

You can eventually gain residency and citizenship through the legal process, and those benefits aren't even the highlights. Legal immigrants, refugees, and asylees may receive many more benefits from the government and community than can undocumented people. They can get help settling into communities, finding jobs, and obtaining proper documentation such as a social security number (SSN) and driver's license. Those who immigrate here legally can also become eligible for federal and state programs such as supplemental security income, nutritional assistance, college and education financial aid, and health insurance. These things can make all the difference when starting a new life.

MOST COMMON TYPES OF VISAS

I have compiled a list of the most common visa types to give you a better understanding of these categories and how to obtain them. For the complete list of visa types, requirements, and application process, visit the U.S. Citizenship and Immigration Services (USCIS) website: *www.uscis.gov.*

Visitor Visa (Non-immigrant, 6 months stay maximum)		
B-1	Temporary business visitors intending to participate in business activities.	*www.uscis.gov/ working-in-the-united-states/ temporary-visitors-for-busines s/b-1-temporary-business-visitor*
B-2	Temporary non-business visitors traveling for vacation, to visit friends/family, seek medical treatment, participate in social events and contests for no pay, or enroll in non-degree recreational courses.	*www.travel.state.gov/ content/travel/en/us-visas/ tourism-visit/visitor.html*

Work Visa (Non-immigrant, 6 years stay maximum)		
H-1B	Persons with at least a bachelor's degree to work in specialty occupations.	*www.uscis.gov/working-in-the-united-states/h-1b-specialty-occupations*
H-2A	Seasonal agricultural workers brought in by U.S. employers.	*www.uscis.gov/working-in-the-united-states/temporary-workers/h-2a-temporary-agricultural-workers*
H-2B	Seasonal non-agricultural workers brought in by U.S. employers.	*www.uscis.gov/working-in-the-united-states/temporary-workers/h-2b-temporary-non-agricultural-workers*
Student & Exchange Visa (Non-immigrant)		
F-1	Students attending primary, secondary, or tertiary school, including language training.	*www.travel.state.gov/content/travel/en/us-visas/study/student-visa.html*
M-1	Students attending vocational and non-academic institutions, excluding language training.	*www.travel.state.gov/content/travel/en/us-visas/study/student-visa.html*
J-1	Individuals participating in work- and study-based exchange visitor programs.	*www.travel.state.gov/content/travel/en/us-visas/study/exchange.html*

Family Sponsored Visa		
K-1	Fianc(é)es of U.S. citizens to marry and live in the U.S.	*www.travel.state.gov/content/travel/en/us-visas/immigrate/family-immigration/nonimmigrant-visa-for-a-fiance-k-1.html*
K-3	Spouses of U.S. citizens waiting on immigrant petitions.	*www.travel.state.gov/content/travel/en/us-visas/immigrate/family-immigration/nonimmigrant-visa-for-a-spouse-k-3.html*
CR-1, IR-1	Spouses of U.S. citizens who have already been issued an immigrant status.	*www.travel.state.gov/content/travel/en/us-visas/immigrate/family-immigration/immigrant-visa-for-spouse.html*
IR-2	Unmarried children, under 21 years of age, of a U.S. citizen.	*www.travel.state.gov/content/travel/en/us-visas/immigrate/family-immigration.html*
IR-2, CR-2, IR-5, F-1, F-3, F-4	Family members and relatives of U.S. citizens.	*www.travel.state.gov/content/travel/en/us-visas/immigrate/family-immigration.html*
F-2A, F-2B	Family members and relatives of lawfully permanent residents.	*www.travel.state.gov/content/travel/en/us-visas/immigrate/family-immigration.html*
Diversity Visa (Immigrant)		
DV-1	Diversity immigrant/ permanent resident.	*www.uscis.gov/green-card/green-card-eligibility/green-card-through-the-diversity-immigrant-visa-program*

In the following sections, we will dive deeper into some of these visas and their application process.

HOW TO IMMIGRATE TO THE U.S. LEGALLY - TYPES OF COMMON VISAS

The visa types below are presented by the relative ease of obtaining and grouped based on similar categories.

CATEGORY: BUSINESS/TOURISM

B-1/B-2: These types of visas are issued to temporary visitors intending to stay for a maximum of six months. B-1 for business purposes, B-2 for tourism and leisure. You can learn more about travel visas here: *www.travel.state.gov/content/travel/en/us-visas/tourism-visit/visitor.html*. These visas are designed to cover most forms of temporary entrance into the United States.

Applicants who wish to receive a B-1, B-2, or a combination of both must be able to provide the following: a passport that is valid for at least six months beyond the end date of their trip, another corresponding piece of photographic ID, and proof of income sufficient enough to fund their return trip.

Additionally, applicants may be vetted on the basis of what type of ties they have to their home country and how likely they are to return home after their allotted time has passed. The United States does its best to ensure this by selecting applicants with (1) apparent motivations to return home (including property ownership, family, a job, etc.)

and (2) a proven track record of adhering to the conditions of previously issued B-1/B-2 visas. For this latter factor, applicants may be asked to provide documentation on their last five trips outside the country including to the United States, if applicable.

Applicants from most countries in the European Union do not have to meet these criteria, and EU residents can travel without a visa for up to 90 days.

Once your B-1/B-2 visa has been granted, you may execute your trip as long as it falls into business or tourist travel categories.

These business objectives fall within the purview of a B-1 visa: finalizing a deal, meeting with clients, attending a conference/niche-specific trade show, and other similar tasks.

Examples of B-2 visa activities are vacation, tourism, visiting a family member, receiving medical treatment, participating in social events, etc.

B-1/B-2 visas cover 180 days in the United States and can be divided into multiple visits as the need arises. Although the initial maximum period is up to six months, the good news is that this period can be extended for an additional six months by filing out form I-539 (Application to Extend/Change Nonimmigrant Status found at *www. uscis.gov/i-539*.

You must file for an extension before your current status expires. USCIS recommends at least 45 days in advance. Otherwise, you may be barred from returning and/or may be removed (deported).

You may find more information on the following page on USCIS's website dedicated to extending non-immigrant stay: *www.uscis.gov/forms/explore-my-options/ extend-my-nonimmigrant-stay*.

It's also worth noting that visitor visas will not be issued for birth tourism, which is the act of traveling to the United States to obtain U.S. citizenship for a child.

CATEGORY: WORK

H-2B: Also known as the temporary non-agricultural work visa, the H-2B visa allows workers within certain fields to enter the United States on a temporary basis. In order to be considered for this visa, the applicant needs an employer willing to sponsor them in an industry that is suffering from a lack of U.S. citizen or green card holder applicants.

Although seasonal in nature, H-2B visas can be extended in year-long increments for an overall total stay of three years, if the employer can prove that their need remains in place and if the immigrant can prove that they still intend to return to their home country at the end of their time in the United States. Upon the expiration of an H2-B visa, the worker has to depart and stay outside the U.S. for at least three months before applying for readmission.

Currently, the United States offers 66,000 H-2B visas annually *(www.uscis.gov/working-in-the-united-states/temporary-workers/h-2b-non-agricultural-workers/ cap-count-for-h-2b-nonimmigrants)*, 33,000 each half of the fiscal year. This can make the application process competitive, with some applicants being rejected because there are not enough visas.

Background work must be done on the part of your employer before an H-2B visa can be granted. The employer must be able to demonstrate that they created a listing for the position in an attempt to hire U.S. citizens before they can begin seeking immigrant applicants. They must then file an I-129 (Petition for a Nonimmigrant Worker) form *(www.uscis.gov/i-129)*, and, if approved, pay several fees on behalf of the specific applicant they intend to hire.

As you are vetted for consideration, it is important to note that you must be able to produce documentation that includes a DS-160 (Nonimmigrant Visa Application) form (*www.travel.state.gov/content/travel/en/us-visas/visa-information-resources/forms/ds-160-online-nonimmigrant-visa-application.html*) for temporary travel to the United States, photo ID (and a corresponding passport), and some form of document that solidifies your intention to return to your country of origin when your visa has expired. This might include the deed to a house or land, a lease agreement, or some other form of proof that you have maintained roots in your home country.

The DS-160 is also used for the fiancé visa.

H-2B visa holders are allowed to bring their family into the country, including unmarried children under the age of 21. These children can attend school while they are in the United States but cannot seek employment.

Follow this link to learn about the H-2B visa: *www.uscis.gov/working-in-the-united-states/temporary-workers/h-2b-temporary-non-agricultural-workers.*

H-1B: The H-1B visa is similar to the H-2B. While the jobs that might qualify for an H-2B visa are broad and generally "unskilled," the H-1B visa is more specific in its qualification requirements. Applicants are expected to hold at least a bachelor's degree that reflects the skills required by the profession they are hoping to enter and demonstrate that they possess said skills.

Most professions that fall within an H-1B visa category involve engineering, math, or legal or medical knowledge.

It is worth noting that the H-1B visa holder's spouse and unmarried children under 21 may also seek admission to the United States.

Like the H-2B visa, the H-1B visa requires the groundwork to be laid by your potential employer. This means that employers must first seek native employees and be able to prove that they weren't able to find any. The employer must then file a series of forms naming the specific applicant as the job recipient. The employer must also be able to prove that they can and will pay wages equal to or exceeding those typical for the industry—in other words, they have to demonstrate that they aren't sourcing immigrant labor to save money.

H-1B visas are limited to 65,000 each fiscal year, though an additional 20,000 slots are made available to applicants with a master's degree or higher. Visas are granted on a three-year basis, with the possibility of extensions to up to six years.

Follow this link to learn more about the H-1B visa type: *www.uscis.gov/working-in-the-united-states/h-1b-specialty -occupations.*

CATEGORY: EXCHANGE VISITORS (STUDENTS/TEACHERS/AU PAIRS/TRAINEES/RESEARCH)

J-1: The J-1 visa exists for visitors that wish to take advantage of an exchange program. Visas are only granted once the applicant has been accepted by an approved exchange organization.

Once you have been accepted by a visitor program, you must complete a DS-160 form and submit yourself for an interview. In most cases, interviews are not required for applicants under the age of 13. Interview exceptions are also usually made for applicants over the age of 80 or for applicants who are simply filing for renewal.

Interviews are held at the United States Embassy in the country in which you currently live. Wait times for your appointment will vary based on availability.

In addition to the aforementioned fees and forms, you must provide a passport and other documentation that can attest to your intentions within the United States (e.g., bank statements, tax returns, financial aid, scholarship paperwork, or documentation from a sponsor). As with all visas, applicants may also be scrutinized based on their intention to return to their country of origin. You will likely be asked to produce some form of documentation attesting to the roots you are maintaining in your country of origin, including, but not limited to, property ownership. In the case that you do not own property, evidence of family ties may be helpful to prove your intention to return to your country of origin.

The validity of J-1 visas varies according to a category, e.g., eighteen months for trainees, five years for research scholars, etc. Once your visa expires, you will be required to return to your country of origin for at least two years before you can seek reentry to the United States unless you are eligible for one of the waivers.

Spouse and unmarried children under 21 are entitled to J-2 visas, including employment authorizations. To apply for employment authorization, the spouse or child will need to file form I-765 (Application for Employment Authorization - (*www.uscis.gov/working-in-the-united-states/information-for-employers-and-employees/employer-information/employment-authorization*.

You may learn more about J-1 visas directly on USCIS's website at *www.uscis.gov/working-in-the-united-states/students-and-exchange-visitors/exchange-visitors*.

CATEGORY: DATING, ENGAGEMENT, & MARRIAGE

K-1: The K-1 visa is also known as a fiancé visa.

If you want to travel to the United States to marry a U.S. citizen, you must get legally married within 90 days after entering the country or risk losing your K-1 status.

Your spouse (U.S. citizen) will need to submit an I-129F (Petition for Alien Fiancé) form *(www.uscis.gov/i-129f)*. Once the I-129F is approved by the National Visa Center (NVC), the form will be forwarded to your local embassy consulate, where you will apply for a K-1 visa. The interview will take place with a Department of State (DOS) officer who will determine your eligibility.

Go to this website to learn about eligibility requirements, process, how to bring in unmarried children under 21 years of age, and more: (*www.uscis.gov/family/ family-of-us-citizens/visas-for-fiancees-of-us-citizens*).

If you are already married, then you are not eligible for a fiancé visa.

IR-1: The IR-1 visa is one of two options for spouses of residents to seek entrance into the United States.

To begin the process, you must be married for at least two years in a way that is legally recognized by the United States.

Couples that meet this criteria must submit a I-130 (Petition for Alien Relatives) form *(www.uscis.gov/i-130)* to the U.S. Citizenship and Immigration Services (USCIS), with the spouse who is a resident filing the petition. Prior to entry into the United States, the applicant must submit to a medical examination that assesses general health and vaccine status. Upon medical approval, the applicant will be interviewed at the United States Embassy of the applicant's country of origin, where the applicant will need to present a passport as well as proof of marriage. Typically, wedding certificates are considered the best way to prove the relationship; however, more informal documentation, including wedding albums, has been accepted at the interviewer's discretion.

The applicant will also be financially responsible for a variety of fees. There are no annual limits placed on IR-1 visas, which tends to speed the process up. The length of time differs from case to case and can't be predicted accurately for individual cases.

CR-1: Similar to the IR-1 visa, CR-1 is for married couples. The difference is that CR-1 is reserved for couples married for less than two years. The application process for CR-1 is similar to IR-1.

Follow this website to learn more about IR-1 and CR-1 visas and their differences: *travel.state.gov/content/travel/en/us-visas/immigrate/family-immigration/immigrant-visa-for-spouse.html.*

CHANGING VISA STATUS

It's worth noting that you are not necessarily forever stuck with the visa that you have now. Although a large amount of confusing or complex information is out there, changing your status is still possible. Even though it can be costly and time-consuming, it is certainly well worth the effort, depending on your situation.

For example, an H-1B holder can become a permanent resident. Permanent residents can become citizens through naturalization. Citizens can file petitions for their immediate family, i.e., fiancé/spouse, children, and parents.

Those interested in pursuing this route will likely find that an immigration lawyer is a suitable avenue for easing the burden of the process.

A friend arrived at the University of Alabama as an F-1 student to study accounting. That's where he met his later-to-be wife, also an F-1 student from India.

After graduation, he relocated to Chicago to work for an accounting firm that would sponsor his visa, and they married. That's when he changed his visa from F-1 to H-1B, and his wife could change her status from F-1 to H-4, apply for Employment Authorization (form I-765), and legally work and support her husband.

Several years later, his permanent resident status was approved, and he finally got his green card, and so did his wife through him. After meeting naturalization requirements, they became citizens.

He now runs his own successful accounting firm and is happily married.

DIVERSITY VISA PROGRAM (GREEN CARD LOTTERY)

WHAT IS THE DV "GREEN CARD" LOTTERY & WHY WAS IT IMPLEMENTED?

The Diversity Immigrant Visa program, also known as the green card lottery, is a United States government program for receiving the United States Permanent Resident Card. The Immigration Act of 1990 established the current and permanent Diversity Visa (DV) program.

The lottery is administered by the Department of State and conducted under the Immigration and Nationality Act (INA). It makes available 55,000 immigrant visas annually and aims to diversify the immigrant population in the United States by selecting applicants from countries with low numbers of immigrants in the previous five years.

It's a federally supported program, and, assuming your country qualifies, you can apply for free at the following website: *www.dvprogram.state.gov.*

The U.S. Department of State's lottery is administered through the Kentucky Consular Center (KCC) in Williamsburg, Kentucky. Although the offices are in Kentucky, the program does not require lottery winners to reside in Kentucky. However, throughout the visa process, you will be in touch with this office.

REQUIREMENTS

Lottery requirements are very specific, allowing for participation only by applicants with citizenship in an eligible country. Those selected must have a high school diploma or at least two years of training.

Lottery winners are also subject to a more general array of immigration requirements. They must be able to show that they do not have a criminal record and prove they have a way to support themselves once they arrive in the country.

Applicants born outside of one approved country may still enter the lottery if they have a spouse or parent from an approved nation. In these situations, applicants must state the approved country on their application.

Note also that requirements are adjusted annually.

Those born in any territory that has sent more than 50,000 immigrants to the United States in the previous five years are not eligible to receive a diversity visa. This figure does not include people who immigrated under special categories such as refugees, asylum seekers, NACARA (Nicaraguan Adjustment and Central American Relief Act) beneficiaries, or previous diversity immigrants.

As stated above, the DV Lottery application is completely free and all online. Just follow this link: *www.dvprogram.state.gov.*

As you fill out the application, ensure you correctly spell all names and double-check the dates and numbers.

Remember, this is an entirely free application. Some companies may try to charge you for this, but if you are computer savvy, you should have all the necessary resources to complete the application without any cost.

The entry timeline is between October and November. Results are usually posted in early May of the following year. Applicants are encouraged to keep their confirmation numbers through September of the following year.

The initial application questions are easy, and you can find a video tutorial by the U.S. Department of State here: *www.youtube.com/watch?v=tOQlh2d2EbQ*.

The U.S. Department of State also has a great resource dedicated to the Diversity Visa Program. It includes detailed information about submitting your application, the selection process, confirming your eligibility/qualifications, interview preparation, interview, submission of all supporting documents, and more. The website can be accessed via the following link: *travel.state.gov/content/travel/en/us-visas/immigrate/diversity-visa-program-entry/diversity-visa-submit-entry1.html*.

YOU WON! CONGRATULATIONS! WHAT'S NEXT, YOU ASK?

Although there might be lawyers and other professional services in your country that specialize in helping you prepare for the interview, you can do all of the required steps yourself. Since you are the one who is pulling all the necessary paperwork for the process, you might as well just compile the materials yourself and save some money.

Having said that, if you don't feel comfortable doing so, then go ahead and seek professional help.

If selected, the notification will come to you via email with further instructions. Keep in mind that it's not yet a guaranteed outcome. Therefore, do not rush; take your time and be thorough with your paperwork. Don't start resigning from your current job and selling all your real estate and other assets prematurely. At least not until you pass the interview.

First, submit your DS-260 form (*www.travel.state.gov/content/travel/en/us-visas/visa-information-resources/forms/online-immigrant-visa-forms/ds-260-faqs.html*). DS-260 is known as the Immigrant Visa and Alien Registration form.

It's important to note that you will need to factor life developments into your application process. For example, if you have a child or get married in the time after you've sent in your application, the record will need to be updated to reflect this.

Adding family members requires the presentation of official documents, so it's best to be prepared. Also, the failure to disclose family members, such as a spouse, will disqualify your entire family from receiving visas.

After submitting form DS-260 online, print the confirmation page. This document is required for your interview. All documents need to be (1) translated correctly, (2) notarized, and (3) sent on time.

Make sure you submit ALL required paperwork.

QUALIFICATIONS

The principal DV applicant must have a high school education or equivalent or two years of qualifying work experience. If you don't have either, you are not eligible. The spouse and children are exempt from this requirement.

High School Education: To qualify as a high school graduate, you must have successfully finished both elementary and secondary education programs that are approximate equivalents to the 12-year system in the United States.

Work Experience: Applicants must have two or more years of work or training experience in the last five years in a job that the U.S. Department of Labor designates as Job Zone 4 or 5, classified with a Specific Vocational Preparation (SVP) rating of 7.0 or higher. To find out more about the U.S. Department of Labor visit the following website *www.onetonline.org*.

Unlike the United Kingdom, Canada, Australia, and New Zealand, the United States does not have English-language proficiency requirements for immigrants.

If you find yourself having trouble meeting deadlines, don't panic. Reach out to the Kentucky Consular Center (KCC) *(www.travel.state.gov/content/travel/en/contact-us/us-visas.html)* to reschedule the interview.

To contact the KCC, make sure that you follow all of their protocols. This includes clearly stating your name, date of birth, and case number at the top of your email. Note that, currently, you can only reach the KCC via phone or email. Paper documents sent to the KCC are unread and disposed of.

The KCC telephone number is 606-526-7500 (7:30 a.m. to 4:00 p.m. EST). The e-mail address is *KCCDV@ state.gov.*

Once your information has been received, you will obtain instructions on scanning and sending whatever additional documentation they require. No further communication will be scheduled until they have received everything they need from you. Once you get an interview scheduled, bring all original documentation with you.

Note that you as the applicant and every family member joining you in the United States will need to submit all required documents:

- Birth certificate
- Marriage certificate, if applicable
- Police reports
- Court records, if applicable

Once you have sent in all the paperwork, you wait for KCC to schedule in-person consular interviews.

After receiving the scheduled interview notification, take the following steps:

- Schedule and complete your medical examination.
- Gather photographs and all remaining required documents. Each DV applicant must bring two (2) identical photos to the interview. Please review the detailed information about photo requirements to ensure that your photos will be acceptable:

www.travel.state.gov/content/travel/en/us-visas/
visa-information-resources/photos.html.

Each applicant will be required to present the following:

- Appointment information, which is printed from the Entrant Status Check on the E-DV website.
- DS-260 confirmation page, which is printed from the Consular Electronic Application Center after completion of the DS-260 application.
- Passport(s) valid for six months beyond the intended U.S. entry date for each family member applying for a visa.
- Original documents or certified copies of civil documents submitted to the KCC. Be prepared to present:

  - Evidence of required DV qualifying education or work experience
  - Deportation documentation
  - Marriage certificate
  - Marriage termination documentation
  - Custody documentation

Before the interview, each applicant must pay the Diversity Visa Lottery fee. This fee is nonrefundable, whether a visa is issued or not.

ADDITIONAL INFORMATION

Can I reschedule my appointment? Diversity Visa issues must be addressed by September 30 of the application year. If, for some reason, you cannot make it to your scheduled appointment, reschedule as soon as possible. Your immigration opportunity can be lost on the basis of missing the September 30 deadline.

After getting our immigrant visas, can I enter the United States on my own with my spouse and children joining me at a later stage? Yes, this is possible, as long as you are the principal applicant. Your family can enter the United States within the allowed time of their immigrant visas.

Can my spouse or children receive diversity visas, even if they were not on my original entry? If you were married or became a parent after submitting your application, you can update your records to reflect the changes to your family. However, if you already had a family that you failed to disclose in your original application, your case will be dismissed, and you will not receive a refund on your fees.

Can my child receive a diversity visa if they turn 21? In most cases, children must be under 21 and unmarried to qualify for a diversity visa. If your child is reaching the cutoff age soon, reach out to the U.S. Embassy immediately, as they may be able to grant you an earlier interview. If your child cannot accompany you on your immigration, you can file a petition. However, it may take a significant amount of time before your child is granted entry.

LITTLE THINGS THAT CAN MAKE A DIFFERENCE

Wear professional attire: Dress nicely, but don't feel the need to appear flashy with excessive jewelry, perfume, etc.

Stay calm and answer all the questions that are asked of you. If you speak English, more power to you, as the interviewing officer will most likely appreciate your fluency in English.

Usually, questions are based on various dates: your husband's birthday, wedding anniversary, etc. Having kids is not a problem, but be prepared for a more intensive screening as the officers' job is to ensure no fraud is committed.

One question you can always expect is, "Why have you decided to come to the U.S.?"

Be sure you have an active and updated U.S. address at which you can receive and easily check for mail. That is where the green card will be sent.

ENTERING THE UNITED STATES

At the moment of entry into the country, the principal applicant must enter first. The visa must be presented at the point of entry to U.S. officials. However, you should note that your entrance to the country will be granted at the discretion of the Department of Homeland Security, even to DV holders. Visa holders can sometimes be denied entry for various reasons, including bad behavior at the border, current travel bans, missing vaccinations, lacking documents, health risks, etc.

Upon your arrival, you will be given a sealed envelope containing the following:

- Your immigration visa petition
- Copies of your identification documents
- Medical exam report
- Affidavit of support
- Waivers (if any)

You have to mail the unsealed package to the address on the envelope. The Department of Homeland Security will also collect your biometrics upon entry.

Begin learning as much as possible when you find out you have won the DV Lottery. As soon as you are admitted into the country, you will be considered a "lawful permanent resident" and, therefore, will have most citizenship rights and be able to work legally. Learning as much of the language and culture beforehand improves your chances of finding employment and can facilitate assimilation.

A hint: Try not to bring everything you own with you. Traveling with too much luggage will be expensive and troublesome. Try to bring only what you need to set yourself up for the first few months. Once you have settled in, you will have ample opportunity to replace the things left behind.

PERMANENT RESIDENTS' RIGHTS & RESPONSIBILITIES

Permanent residents have most of the rights that U.S. citizens do. One of the primary differences is that permanent residents cannot vote in federal elections, participate in jury duty, or run for office.

If you are a male between 18 and 25, be sure to register with the Selective Service System. All male citizens and residents are required to do so, though it should be noted that the country has not seen a draft since the Vietnam War. Failing to register with Selective Services may negatively affect your naturalization process.

Note that you must register with Selective Services even if your immigration case is pending, and you are still waiting for a decision. Visit the Selective Services website to find out more *www.sss.gov*.

You are also required to carry proof of your permanent resident status at all times with you if you are 18 years or older.

Be sure to live in the U.S. for over six months each year. Failing to do so without legitimate reasons (i.e., caring for a family member, attending school, etc.) may be considered abandoning your status.

If you know you will be outside the States for more than twelve months, apply for a reentry permit before leaving the States. You will need to fill out Form I-131, Application for a Travel Document, (*www.uscis.gov/i-131*), and pay a fee. The reentry permit is valid for up to two years.

Your permanent resident card is valid for 10 years, and you must renew it before it expires. To replace or renew your card, you must file Form I-90, Application to Replace Permanent Resident Card, (*www.uscis.gov/i-90*), and pay the fee.

NATURALIZATION & CITIZENSHIP

The pinnacle of the entire immigration process is naturalization, the process of becoming a U.S. citizen. The day you naturalize and take the oath will most likely be one of the most memorable days of your life.

An array of new benefits will open up for you when you become a citizen.

One of those is being able to travel with a U.S. passport. The power of this "blue" passport is vast. You will notice how much easier traveling will become for you as a U.S. citizen. Over half of the world's countries won't require a travel visa if you travel with a U.S. passport.

Upon your return to the States, you will go through the expedited citizens' line.

Another great benefit is that you are given priority when petitioning to bring your family members permanently to the U.S. The process of bringing in immediate family members will become easier and quicker.

After becoming a citizen, you can vote, run for office, serve on jury duty, obtain government benefits, and more.

So, what are the requirements for naturalization?

1. Continuous residence: You must reside in the States for a specific time. Most people have five years (or three if married to a U.S. citizen) of permanent residency. The date when you become permanent, usually the date indicated on your green card, is when your five-year period begins.

2. Physical presence: Before applying, you must be physically present in the States for at least 30 months in the last five years. The requirement time frame drops to 18 months if married to a U.S. citizen in the previous three years.

3. Good moral character: You must demonstrate that you have behaved legally and in an acceptable manner.

4. English and civics: You must know basic English and be able to pass U.S. history and government tests.

Maintaining continuous residence in the States is one of the major requirements. We all know that circumstances change, and we may be required to stay outside of the country for an extended period. If you know you will be outside of the States for one year or longer, apply to preserve your status as an immigrant to pursue naturalization by submitting Form N-470, Application to Preserve Residence for Naturalization Purposes, (*www.uscis.gov/n-470*).

Once the minimum citizenship requirements are met, you can apply by filling out the N-400, Application for Naturalization, (*www.uscis.gov/n-400*) and pay the fee.

USCIS has great resources dedicated to the citizenship process, which can be accessed following this link: *www.uscis.gov/citizenship*.

Follow this link to access an instructional video explaining the account creation and application process: *www.uscis.gov/citizenship/apply-for-citizenship*.

There is also a Form M-476, Guide to Naturalization, by the USCIS: *www.uscis.gov/sites/default/files/document/guides/M-476.pdf*.

USCIS regularly holds free information sessions for the public that help permanent residents and those interested in naturalization learn about the process, including eligibility, test questions, rights, and responsibilities. You can access the free naturalization sessions calendar and sign up via *www.uscis.gov/citizenship/learners/free-information-sessions*.

Here are two other great resources to check out prior to or during the application process:

USA Learns - *www.usalearns.org/#citizen*
Citizenshipworks - *www.citizenshipworks.org*

You will find many YouTube videos that can help prepare for the interview, i.e., mock interviews, test questions, minimum required paperwork suggestions, etc. Various applications can even help prepare for the test via questions and answers, flashcards, true-false checks, etc.

Then comes the big day: the *Naturalization Interview*.

It's recommended you wear professional attire and arrive early. If possible, don't even wear perfume, as some officers may not like the particular smell or even be allergic.

Make sure you are prepared for the civics test and thoroughly review your application.

The officer will ask for sets of documents to verify your identity and will proceed to the oath, where you swear to tell the truth and nothing but the truth.

Some officers will start with civics, and the others with asking questions related to your background. There is no right or wrong order. Be familiar with every date and fact you have put into your application.

The officers are trained to detect lies, and their questions can be deceiving. Their goal is to ensure that citizenship is given to the person with the right moral character who will most likely contribute in positive ways to U.S. society. Be honest about your past, including any new or past administrative and criminal interactions with law enforcement. If you had previous weapons training experience, disclose it if asked.

Remember that USCIS has done an intensive background check on you before inviting you to the interview. Do not lie during the interview, as lying to an officer can be grounds for denial.

There is no single factor that can result in approval or a denial of your application. The U.S. knows that we can't change the past but can change the future. This is another thing that I like about this country. The entire persona is thoroughly reviewed to determine the person's moral character.

There are many cases of approvals despite past encounters with law enforcement, assuming that the officer is persuaded that the person has now changed.

Sometimes, the officer may ask for more time to review the case and/or request additional documentation before making the final decision. Thank the officer before leaving and be sure to comply with any requirements and to not miss any deadlines. If the decision has not been made on the spot, it will come in the mail and be posted on your USCIS online portal.

After receiving approval, you will be scheduled to attend a ceremony and take the Oath of Allegiance. The Oath Ceremony is a big day worthy of celebration. This is the day when you want to be dressed up and take plenty of pictures. This is the day you want to remember.

In many cases, you are allowed to bring your closest family members to the oath ceremony. If unsure, check with your local immigration office.

Please note that you are not a citizen until you have taken the Oath of Allegiance.

After taking your oath, take a day off and pat yourself on the shoulder. Celebrate. You have just achieved a huge and notable milestone.

As with many things in life, citizenship comes with responsibilities. Below are some noteworthy ones:

- Defend and support the Constitution and the United States.
- Respect and obey federal, state, and local laws.
- Pay taxes on time.
- Serve on a jury.
- Participate in the democratic process and respect the rights, opinions, and beliefs of others.

I like to look at citizenship as a privilege. Privileges are granted and can be taken away in certain circumstances. Below are some of the reasons for which citizenship can be revoked:

- If naturalization was procured illegally (this means that you were not eligible for naturalization in the first place).
- If a person intentionally tried to deceive officials, misrepresented themself, or failed to disclose facts

during the naturalization process or the following examination.

- If a person became affiliated with or became a member of a totalitarian party or terrorist organization within five years of the naturalization.
- If a person became naturalized on the basis of service in the U.S. armed forces and was dishonorably discharged.

I am certain that none of the above-mentioned are relevant for the vast majority as we immigrated to the United States with good intentions.

If you are already a naturalized citizen, I want to congratulate you on reaching a significant milestone. Let this landmark be one of many of your noteworthy achievements!

ILLEGAL IMMIGRATION

Undocumented immigration, also known as illegal immigration, has long been a point of contention among Americans. Many people in the country are supportive of helping immigrants make better lives here, recognizing that the U.S. got its start through immigration, was built largely by immigrants, and continues to benefit from them. However, others merely see immigrants as the "Other," people invading the country, "stealing" jobs, and disrupting the comfortable homogeneity of their lives. Sometimes, being against undocumented immigration is just a guise for these people to prevent all forms of immigration.

So, what exactly constitutes illegal? There are three main ways to become classified as unlawfully present in the U.S.

Number one, it is a common assumption that undocumented immigrants *cross the border* on foot and obtain jobs that pay them under the table, hence the effort to build a wall along the southern border with Mexico.

Those crossing the border without prior permission often have no way of knowing beforehand whether they will be granted access. Asylum must be requested at the border or within the U.S., making planning ahead nearly impossible. Making the request from the border is the ideal method in terms of legality, but it is often so difficult that people resort to attempting an unauthorized crossing.

Number two, people who obtain documentation or *bribe* those in the right places to fly into the country constitute a type of undocumented immigration that disregards federal immigration laws from the get-go.

Number three, immigrants who *overstay* their authorized period or violate the terms of entry become illegal. For example, immigrants who enter the country as tourists but then proceed to work or enroll in classes are seen as having overstayed or violated their terms of entry if they do not properly change their visa status from tourist to student visa.

Even with the best of intentions, it can be easier than expected for your status to slip into "illegal." Many immigrants try their hardest to follow the law to the letter but still find themselves tangled up in a legal nightmare. Such entanglements can happen while seeking asylum through the courts or can happen after years of residing in the U.S.

due to a small mistake such as letting your documents expire. You must remain vigilant at all points of the process to maintain the best chances of success.

PATH TO LEGALIZATION FOR UNDOCUMENTED IMMIGRANTS

While seeking legalization as an undocumented immigrant is not easy, it can be accomplished in one of these ways:

- **Marriage**: Undocumented immigrants can become legalized by marrying a U.S. citizen and going through the necessary immigration process.

- **Asylum**: Though asylum seekers are not offered immediate citizenship, they are granted a narrow path toward it. The United States grants asylum to incoming immigrants who are able to prove that they would be risking their lives if they were to return to their home country.

  Said risk must be attributable to persecution that is being made based on race, religion, nationality, or political opinion. Once granted asylum, immigrants can apply for a green card.

- **U Visa**: This visa is reserved for victims of qualified crime who aid law enforcement. Congress signed this into law in October 2000, intending to encourage noncitizen victims to work with prosecutors and officers without fear of being deported. The law "rewards" illegals who suffered mental or physical abuse from a qualifying criminal activity. More information, including a list of qualifying criminal activities, can be found following this link: *www.uscis.gov/humanitarian/victims-of-human-trafficking-and-other-crimes/victims-of-criminal-activity-u-nonimmigrant-status.*

Many undocumented immigrants find Immigration and Customs Enforcement (ICE) officers frightening. Know that even as an undocumented immigrant, your rights[3][4][5][6] allow you to take the following actions:

- Refuse to open the door unless ICE agents have a valid search warrant signed by a judge or if the warrant doesn't have your correct name and address.

- Refuse to allow ICE officers inside your house if they only have the ICE deportation warrant and do not have a search warrant signed by a judge.

---

[3]   "Know Your Rights | Immigrants' Rights | American Civil Liberties Union." https://www.aclu.org/know-your-rights/immigrants-rights. Accessed 3 Dec. 2022.

[4]   "Know Your Rights: If ICE Visits Your Home." https://pennstatelaw.psu.edu/sites/default/files/documents/pdfs/Immigrants/Home_Customize.pdf. Accessed 3 Dec. 2022.

[5]   "Your Rights at Home and at Work - National Immigration Law Center." https://www.nilc.org/get-involved/community-education-resources/know-your-rights/imm_enfrcmt_homework_rts_2008-05-2/. Accessed 3 Dec. 2022.

[6]   "Know Your Rights with ICE - Immigrant Defense Project." https://www.immigrantdefenseproject.org/know-your-rights-with-ice/. Accessed 3 Dec. 2022.

- Remain silent and refuse to show identity documents that say what country you are from. If you choose to stay silent, say it out loud.

- Refuse to answer questions about how you entered the States and where you were born.

- Refuse to move if agents ask you to stand in a group according to immigration status or move to an area not designated for a particular group.

- Refuse a search if stopped for questioning but not arrested. Officers may legally "pat down" your clothes if they suspect you have a weapon.

- Speak to a lawyer if taken into custody or detained. If you do not have a lawyer, ask the officer for a list of pro bono lawyers.

- Refuse to sign any paperwork until you speak to a lawyer.

Just because you don't have legal status (yet), don't think you are "disabled." Many undocumented immigrants cut themselves short simply because they don't have legal paperwork. Excuses such as if I only had an SSN, I would have bought my first house instead of renting for years and years, I would have started my business had I been legal in this country, I can't go to school to improve my skills because my papers are not correct, etc.

The story below demonstrates that you don't have to be forever stuck in one place. While some things are outside our control, others are still within it. As they say, if there is a will, there is a way. Creativity, outside-of-the-box thinking, and adaptability can do wonders.

A friend from a Latin American country was smuggled into the U.S. across the Mexican border by a coyote. During the transit, somewhere in Mexico, a gang unaffiliated with the coyote managed to take her brother hostage (from a bus station, which was a mutual rendezvous point). The mother (then in the U.S.), on top of already paying a hefty fee to the coyote for the trip and so-called "protection," was now forced to pay the ransom to the other gang as well so the son wouldn't get harmed.

At only 13 years of age, she had to swim across the Rio Grande (a river along the U.S.-Mexico border) at her own risk. Upon crossing the U.S. border, she was detained by the U.S. border patrol , and her uncle (who was accompanying her) fled in sight of the customs and border protection officers.

She was detained and released to her mother after several days. One can only imagine the shock and fear this little girl had to endure. To this day, she remembers the holding cell being cold and her getting lice ("little animals" in her own words) from the other inmates.

Like many from that part of the region, they fled gang violence and extreme poverty. Based on this, the family applied for asylum. Ten years later, she finally received her social security number (SSN) and work authorization. She is now in line for permanent residency.

During this time, she attended school and helped her family financially by working odd jobs where she could learn new skills that allowed her to start her own company later. She is now a promising young entrepreneur who also happens to be happily married.

Don't let the circumstances define you.

Congratulations on finishing Chapter 2!

Use the following questions to help you reflect on the chapter you just read.

1. Which 3 visa types do you think you meet the requirements for or could qualify for?

2. What immigration application process requirements can you readily or easily obtain?

3. List down persons you personally know who have successfully immigrated to the U.S. They may be able to offer insight and advice with your application.

Your progress so far   15%

2/13

CHAPTER 3

LAW & ORDER

BASIC RIGHTS & SOCIAL SERVICES

Here, we will learn about the fundamental rights, social services, and some important documentation and identification you must obtain to work and travel freely. Most importantly, you will learn about what pitfalls to avoid and what not to do.

It's important to realize that, as an immigrant, you have the same basic rights as any citizen. The United States Constitution often uses the term "people" or "persons" rather than "citizen(s)," highlighting that the rights it outlines are human rights, not uniquely American citizen rights. This means that immigrants have just as much right to due process of law in criminal cases, as citizens do, granting them fair treatment through the normal judicial system of the United States, as stated by the Fifth Amendment. The Sixth Amendment then grants immigrants the right to the assistance of counsel for defense in said due process, meaning the right to a lawyer.

Yet, the language used in the Constitution and in legal matters generally can be tricky. Notice that the two above rights refer to criminal cases. Many court cases that immigrants face, such as deportation proceedings, are actually not criminal cases, but rather civil cases. In civil cases, the right to legal counsel often does not apply; the government is only required to provide counsel if the person is accused of a felony. However, the first offense of crossing the border illegally is only a misdemeanor, meaning a legal counsel may not be provided. All of this is to say: if you find yourself with a deportation issue, you will need to seek out an immigration lawyer on your own and be responsible for all associated expenses.

It's worth mentioning that since my arrival, I have not been stopped a single time without a valid reason. Nor have I been asked for identification or detained by authorities without probable cause, regardless of the time of the day or my whereabouts. I have also never witnessed a police officer requesting a bribe or conducting illegal activity. Throughout decades of running businesses, no auditor or person of power has ever threatened to shut down my company or demanded a bribe. This alone is worth a lot.

As with rights and services, all laws in the U.S. apply to everyone. Some are obvious, like laws against robbery or murder. But you might not be aware of some of the others, or just not very familiar with their details.

TAX LAW

It is important to keep track of taxes every year. Every immigrant, documented or otherwise, has the same obligation as any citizen to pay taxes. This means paying taxes as an individual, as well as for any companies or business entities you might have. Even if you work very little, you will still usually need to pay taxes. The best way to know for sure is to try to pay them, and if you don't need to, then you will find out from the Internal Revenue Service or IRS (*www.irs.gov*).

In most cases, if you do need to pay, you will receive a form from your employer, either a 1099 or a W-2. These documents provide pertinent income information for tax preparation. You may find it helpful to consult an accountant when preparing your tax information. For a fee, an accountant should be able to help you get all of your legal ducks in a row.

Some immigrants wonder why they should pay taxes if they have no money left, or why money sent back to their country of origin is taxable. This relates to the fundamental reasons behind paying taxes. Taxes fund public goods and services, such as roads and public schools for children, which are available to everyone. If you are sending money back to another country, this doesn't change the fact that you're using services in the U.S., and those services need to be paid for somehow. So taxes take priority as the payment you need to make to live in the U.S., and then any extra money can be spent however you wish on yourself and your family in any country. It's also important to note that paying your taxes in a timely manner can be a major benefit when it comes to your legalization. Immigrants who can prove that they pay their taxes will have a much better chance of being accepted than those who can't.

Paying taxes comes right after paying essential living expenses such as lodging and food. Everything else comes next. If you're not sending money to other people yet and still don't have enough money to pay taxes, you may either be mismanaging your money or legitimately not earning enough. If the latter, you should be eligible for assistance from the government. In later chapters, we will cover some of these benefits in more detail. By utilizing the benefits wisely, you can gain the momentum to recover. The quicker you get back up, the better it is, as government aid is only a temporary measure. As Muhammad Ali once said, "There's nothing wrong with getting knocked down, as long as you get right back up."

Just like how you must pay taxes on the income you make in the U.S., you might still be required to pay taxes on income from overseas. If you have assets abroad, you fall under FBAR (Foreign Bank and Financial Accounts) and/or 8938 regulations. These regulations require you to disclose these assets to the U.S. government, with consequences of up to $60,000 in fines if you fail to disclose the information, as well as potential criminal penalties. Any of these consequences could hurt your immigration status, therefore it's advisable to follow the tax protocol.

In early 2010, Javier, a Puerto Rican, rented a room with us. He had recently relocated to Baltimore after going through a painful and dramatic divorce.

He was driving this beautiful white `07 Mercedes Benz E Class. His financing APR (annual percentage rate) was well over 20% for the used car.

I later came to find out that he had to claim Chapter 7 bankruptcy after being audited by the IRS for not paying taxes. You see, the IRS does backdated audits. He was audited for the three years of unpaid taxes, the amount owed to the government was established, and backdated interest was applied. The money owed snowballed to the point Javier was forced to seek bankruptcy.

Chapter 7 stays on a credit report for up to ten years. Any potential creditor who sees this in your credit history will be greatly concerned and consider you a higher risk, which will cost you more for any credit given. The logic is if they are taking on a higher-risk portfolio/persona, their potential return should be higher as well, basic risk-reward ratio. Therefore, if approved, expect to pay a lot more interest. Money immediately gets more expensive for those who have filed for bankruptcy, so your purchasing power drastically drops.

Luckily for Javier, he is a Puerto Rican, and Puerto Ricans are U.S. citizens. For us immigrants, the risk is even greater. Not paying or evading taxes may not only cost more financially but also negatively affect our immigration status. Be mindful.

SOCIAL SECURITY NUMBER (SSN)

Another uniquely American legal matter is the social security number (SSN). I recall calling my cousin in Maryland, begging him to take me away from the harsh slave-like conditions I found myself in upon my initial arrival to the United States (in Colorado). He suggested I wait for my

SSN to arrive since I had already applied for it. Without fully realizing the power of an SSN, I cried aloud to him, asking him to take me out of this "captivity," and said I wouldn't need that number. Looking back now, I see how ignorant I was. Your SSN is one of the most critical numbers you will ever have to remember.

Each SSN is nine digits long, consisting of three parts like so:123-45-6789. Every citizen, permanent resident, and temporary working resident of the U.S. is issued a unique SSN, which acts as a national identification number for keeping track of taxes, social security benefits, gaining employment, and other legal matters. It is issued on just a small paper card; ironic, considering it is one of the most important documents that people in the U.S. possess, right up there with a birth certificate.

Replacing it is possible yet requires gathering documentation, applying for a replacement, and visiting the appropriate offices. It's worth mentioning that you are limited to three replacements in a year and ten during your lifetime.

Here is the link to find out the exact steps you need to take to replace your lost SSN card: *www.ssa.gov/ssnumber/ ss5doc.htm*.

It took me some time to understand the significance of having an SSN number. When I arrived in the United States, I immediately found myself in an awful situation, working without compensation under indentured conditions. I remember almost begging my cousin over the phone to fly me out of Denver to Baltimore (where he was residing) despite his advice to first wait for my SSN number to be issued. SSN is one of the most important numbers you will have. The SSN is used to identify an individual's financial and background information. Which means it will be asked of you many times. Examples include getting a new phone, applying to open a bank account, purchasing a house, and before being considered for employment.

Indeed, many people entering the United States are met with conditions scarcely better than what they'd left behind. Escaping these situations is possible, and getting an SSN is a crucial part of that process.

Here is how to apply for an SSN number:

- Obtain proper identification. Various accepted forms of identification include a driver's license, a passport, a birth certificate, or a religious record showing the time and place of your birth.
- Print and fill out the application.
- Take or mail the application to the local SSN branch.

Here is the link for more information about Social Security Number and Card: *www.ssa.gov/ssnumber.*

When you receive your card, be sure to memorize the number immediately. Do not share the number with anyone unless you are absolutely certain you know the identity of the party requesting it. Usually only the government and your bank need to see it. Billions of dollars are lost every year to criminals stealing peoples' social security numbers, so guard yours with your life.

It's also worth noting that laminating your card is forbidden, so keep it in a dry, safe place.

INDIVIDUAL TAXPAYER IDENTIFICATION NUMBER (ITIN):

If you do not qualify for an SSN number, you may still be able apply for an ITIN number. Working with an ITIN and paying your taxes is better than working for cash, especially when the time comes for legalization.

An ITIN is available for some nonresident and resident aliens, including their spouses, and dependents who don't qualify for an SSN.

Like SSNs, ITINs also consist of 9 digits. ITINs start with the numeral "9" and are formatted the same as SSNs (123-45-6789).

To get an ITIN you must complete form W-7, IRS Application for Individual Taxpayer Identification Number *(www.irs.gov/forms-pubs/about-form-w-7)*. The form will require foreign status and proof of identity.

Here is the link to apply: *www.irs.gov/individuals/how-do-i-apply-for-an-itin.*

Just by having an ITIN, your chances of finding employment increase. I know people that were able to find jobs in daycare facilities, offices, restaurants, and elsewhere by presenting their ITINs since they didn't have SSNs.

Most employers don't like paying with cash because it is almost non-traceable and it doesn't allow them to write off those expenses.

DRIVER'S LICENSE

I come from Tashkent, which is a very densely populated city in Uzbekistan. Public transportation is safe and convenient. Living in Tashkent, I didn't need to own a car.

Except for the large metropolitan areas such as New York, a car will probably be necessary to ensure reliable transportation in the U.S. In smaller cities and towns, you will be almost required to drive to get to your destination in time. To that end, learning how to drive (for those who do not already) can be very helpful as you prepare for your move.

Besides public transportation, you may also take advantage of traditional cab services and on-demand ride-hailing applications like Uber and Lyft. Some will even have ride-sharing/carpooling features to save on transportation costs. These services are generally reliable and accessible per request in many parts of the States regardless of the time of day. The only caveat is that the cost will quickly add up if you keep relying on these means only.

If you have never had a driver's license before, you will need to look into your state's motor vehicle administration (MVA) or department of motor vehicle (DMV) requirements. Most states will require you to complete a driver's education program. In general, the minimum age for a full unrestricted license varies between 16 and 18, depending on the state. You will also need to pass the vision test, provide required paperwork such as proof of legal residency, pay a fee, and pass theoretical and practical driving tests.

Don't get discouraged if you don't pass the tests the first time. After failing my third attempt at my driving test, I still clearly remember my cousin telling me with a smile on his face that he would put me on a plane back to Uzbekistan if I failed again. I must admit that his scare tactics worked, as the very next time I passed.

If you are already here and know how to drive, get your U.S. driver's license as soon as you can. Not only will it give you the right to drive, but it can also be used for identification purposes. In this country, a driver's license is the ID you will have to carry with you unless you are traveling outside of the country.

Depending on state laws and regulations, in most cases, your out-of-country license is good, in general, for 30 to 90 days. Some states may require you to have an International Driving Permit or IDP *(www.usa.gov/visitors-driving)* and valid driver's license from your own country. You can find out the ID requirements of the state where you will be driving via the following link: *www.usa.gov/motor-vehicle-services.* The clock generally starts from the date of entry into America. The best way to find out is to call or go online to your state's DMV website.

On top of safety and convenience, having a vehicle will provide you with freedom to travel great distances quickly. Cars also allow you the option to search for jobs outside your immediate neighborhood. Your family members, friends, or neighbors may offer you a ride, but that isn't a long-term solution if you want to settle down and start a new life.

It's important you always have your driver's license, vehicle registration, and insurance card with you whenever operating a motor vehicle. You will frequently be asked to show your driver's license as a form of ID, so carry it at all times.

One of the unusual things that stood out compared to driving in Uzbekistan was the school bus rule; whenever its red lights flashed and stop signs (on the sides of the bus) were put up, all cars on both sides of the road must stop as the bus is either dropping off or picking up children.

The other one was the ability to turn right on red after a complete stop.

Of course, there are many other rules, and some vary state by state. Therefore, familiarize yourself with the laws specific to your state before you get behind the wheel.

Visit this website to learn how to get a driver's license or to renew it, register your vehicle, and access other vehicle-related services: *www.usa.gov/motor-vehicle-services.*

It's worth mentioning that hitchhiking is not common in the States, and in many places, it's illegal. For your safety, it's not recommended to hitchhike or give rides to hitchhikers.

DRINKING & DRIVING

Driving is a privilege in America, not a right. Remember that before you get behind the wheel intoxicated. The privilege of driving can be taken away.

While consuming alcohol is legal for adults age 21 and over, issues arise when driving is involved. During my time in the United States, I witnessed the consequences of driving under the influence (DUI)—a term that describes having more alcohol in your system than the law allows. Not only are DUI convictions expensive, they require a lot of time and energy to overcome. DUIs and other citations usually stay on your record forever and may impact employment opportunities.

DUIs can be avoided by monitoring your consumption, arranging for a ride, or taking advantage of ride-sharing services such as Uber or Lyft. Play it safe. Drinking and driving is dangerous and never worth the risk.

INTERACTIONS WITH LAW ENFORCEMENT

Different cultures have their own way of interacting with the police. For example, where I am from, it is considered a sign of respect to get out of the car and present yourself to the officer. In the United States, this would likely be seen as a sign of aggression unless the officer explicitly tells you to do so. In America, if the police pull you over, all you have to do is roll down your window and wait for the officer to approach you. Keeping your hands on the steering wheel is also recommended. Avoid making sudden movements. The very first thing the officer will do is ask for your driver's license, registration card (proof of the vehicle ownership), and proof of automobile insurance. Stay calm and comply with the officer's instructions at all times.

I also have heard stories of a victim being severely beaten and sometimes killed for trying to fight off thieves. It's important to always keep your car doors locked, stay alert, especially in places you are not yet familiar with and do not resist if confronted by a gang or threatened with a knife and/or gunpoint. Material things are not worth your health or life. If robbed, do not pursue the robber. If assaulted, do not try to make it right by punishing the person who assaulted you. Instead, report it to the police and let the authorities handle it. The last thing you would want is the person attacking, calling the police on you, and presenting him/her as a victim and you as an aggressor.

I have witnessed guys who got into a bar fight taken away by authorities for not complying with their demands and bullying or trying to fight back the police.

If in a domestic argument with your other half or a friend, I would try to cool down and think twice before reporting an incident to the police. A domestic charge affects the future of your entire family, income, job status, including your immigration, and naturalization. I am not saying you should take a beating if the other side is aggressive or that you should stay silent, especially in life-threatening situations. Just be truthful and don't over-exaggerate. It is fine to disagree and argue as long as it is not abusive and repeated. Know that once authorities arrive, they will listen to both sides and most likely will end up taking one party into custody and pressing charges. If that were to happen, this would cost unneeded aggravation, additional bills dealing with an attorney, fines, and legal fees, not to mention a negative strike against one's record and friendship or relationship, which is now even more difficult to amend.

One other thing to mention is that law enforcement works effectively in this country. And you don't have to bribe someone to get your rights defended. If you ever find yourself in a situation needing help from authorities, don't hesitate to call them.

Dial 911 for emergencies, whether fire, health, or law-enforcement-related. For non-emergency situations, reporting, and/or information, dial 411.

Remember, the place to prove your legal point is in court. In no case should you argue with a law enforcement officer, even if you are certain you're in the right.

TRIBAL TRUST

People coming from the same parts of the planet tend to place significant trust in one another once they get to the United States. While tribal trust can help you establish roots in your new country, it also leaves immigrants vulnerable to manipulation.

Imagine yourself as an immigrant with money but without the proper documents to purchase a home in the United States. You don't know many people except a mutual friend who is also from your own country of origin. This friend shares the same language and background as you and has the legal standing to buy a house. You do all the work of finding the house and covering all expenses such as down payment, closing costs, insurance, taxes, etc. And your friend stands to purchase it.

After happily living in your dream home for years, your trusted "friend" shows up at the front door one day, demanding you to pack and leave. Suddenly, you find yourself in an extremely confusing and frustrating situation. Unfortunately, your friend is completely within his legal rights because his name is on the deed, not yours.

The same situation could happen in business or any other arrangement secured with a handshake instead of legal documents. Moral of the story: trust is great, but when it comes to personal finance, make sure you are backing it up with a contract put together by a professional.

A guy I know immigrated to the States with cash from liquidating his businesses and property back home. Unfortunately, he didn't speak the language and didn't know how to run a business in America. In one of the Uzbek gatherings, he met a "local" guy who had been here for some time, knew the language, and pretended to know how to run a business. They shook hands and, in rather quick fashion, decided to go into the logistics business together. The company was formed under the local guy's name, and several expensive long-haul trucks were purchased. The newcomer provided all the funding where the local guy was supposed to run the business. Shortly after, the local guy booted the newcomer out of the business. Unfortunately for the newcomer, this was possible because his name was not on any of the legal documents.

I am not trying to discourage you from doing business with those who are from your neck of the woods. I have plenty more examples where these partnerships were successful. In fact, you may find that communication with those from your country is easier due to you sharing the same background, ethics, and, obviously, language. Therefore, these unions may be strong, successful, and lasting. What I am suggesting is to be cautious and to formalize these agreements legally.

Congratulations on finishing Chapter 3!

Use the following questions to help you reflect on the chapter you just read.

1. What are 3 things legal in your country but illegal or frowned upon in the U.S.?

2. Find the speed limits for each type of road in your top 3 States based on your answers in Chapter 1.

3. What are the consequences of driving under the influence in your home country compared to the U.S.?

Your progress so far   23%

3/13

CHAPTER 4

CULTURE SHOCK & OTHER PITFALLS IMMIGRANTS FACE

My immigrant friend, you may find this chapter somewhat surprising and perhaps even astonishing, as I have gathered a list of items that may seem awkward for a newcomer. These are the things that stood out for me and took a bit of acclimation before they either settled with me or eventually became part of the new me.

After the mountains of paperwork, legal battles, costly trips, and potentially more arduous struggles associated with getting to the U.S., you will likely face challenges once you're here and settling in. Indeed, for many, the struggles may feel as though they will never end.

There was a point during my early days in the U.S. where I easily could have packed up and left. Six months into my time here, I felt so homesick that the only thing keeping me from leaving was the need to repay a loan to my older brother, Anvar, and my ego. I was experiencing culture shock—which for me was a sense of isolation so severe that I could hardly take it anymore. But I knew I wouldn't be at peace with myself if I returned with unpaid debt and unrealized dreams. It would mean a total defeat.

Looking back, I am grateful for the debt that kept me here. I stayed long enough to get used to the United States. My surroundings became increasingly familiar, and my social and business circle grew. I started enjoying and appreciating American traits such as friendliness, fairness, and patience while enjoying solid infrastructure, abundance, peace, superiority, and equality of law. It took time, but slowly, the U.S. began to feel like home.

How well you adjust will typically depend on many factors, such as your cultural background, your perception of your move to the U.S., and your mindset. If you come from a similar country, perhaps somewhere in Europe or even a large city in another country, life in the U.S. might not feel so different. And if you have been waiting for this moment for years, full of anticipation, then perhaps you feel excited and ready to settle into your new American life.

This feeling of elation is common and something to take advantage of. Some call it the *Honeymoon Phase* of culture shock--a period in which experiencing something new and different after all your hard work leads to a feeling of euphoria. But as its name suggests, it doesn't generally last forever. And if you hadn't looked forward to arriving in the U.S. in the first place, or perhaps the journey here was traumatic, then this stage might not be waiting for you. You might skip straight to what is often called the *Aggravation Phase.*

When this hits, usually after a few months, cultural differences can start to become more apparent and even glaring. You may begin comparing U.S. culture to that of your country of origin, finding the differences frustrating or even painful.

Language barriers can further accentuate the problem as you struggle to communicate socially and in your place of work. From minor chores like transactions with cashiers to more critical tasks like following up on legal matters, all of this can easily lead to a feeling of isolation, but don't give up. Integrating into the community is key to raising yourself out of this swampy state of mind.

This can even mean seeking out people with similar backgrounds to yourself, as many cities and even small towns will have groups of immigrants from around the world. But, in the long term, it's best not to limit yourself to what you know. After all, why not take this opportunity to expand your horizons and reach your full potential since you are already here? The best way to do that is to fully mix with the community, immersing yourself in the new culture and language. It might feel like jumping into a cold swimming pool, but it warms up as soon as you start to move around. It's particularly important to immerse children, as they can pick up a new language within just a few months if given a chance, helping them immediately integrate and flourish in their new lives.

Adjustment tends to set in somewhere between six months and a year. In the *Integration Phase*, you start to leave feelings of resentment and aggravation behind. You begin settling into a routine, accepting your new environment, and even solving some nagging problems.

With enough time and effort, you'll reach the *Bi-Cultural Phase*, where you feel like part of your new culture. You likely haven't left your old culture entirely behind, and indeed you don't ever need to. Even after reaching the *Independence Phase*, it's more than possible to embrace both cultures, giving time for each and enjoying their differences. But you will have enough experience with your new culture that it no longer feels new.

Nevertheless, pain points can still crop up from time to time. Globalization has created a sense of tension in the United States. Some—though certainly not all—U.S. citizens view immigrants with hostility, forming assumptions based on accents or skin tones. These attitudes make it difficult to acclimate socially and can also create bumps in the legal process.

And, of course, you may also continue to encounter material concerns. For example, language barriers can persist, and local friendships may prove challenging to foster. Other concerns, like a lack of reliable transportation or decent clothing, may also contribute to an ongoing sense of cultural disorientation. However, these concerns may decrease as you find work and are able to begin supporting yourself.

CULTURAL DIFFERENCES

No matter your country of origin, cultural differences will exist. My home country, Uzbekistan, is a country with a culture that runs deep. Upon entering the United States, I was surprised to encounter differences in many things, including handshaking, eye contact and smiling, dating, and much more.

HANDSHAKING

Uzbekistan was once part of the USSR and remains influenced by Russian culture. Therefore, in Uzbekistan, people greet one another by extending their right hand for a shake, which is believed to signify neither party is armed. In fact, declining a handshake is a sign of mistrust or displeasure.

In the U.S., I found things to be quite different. Even my roommate, Steve, would never extend his hand. He would only say "hi" or "bye," which was the most you could expect from him. At first, I thought this was good practice as it eliminates the exchange of germs.

However, I've since come to understand there is power in shaking hands. As I have gone up the ladder, I've noticed that successful people make a point of shaking hands and maintaining eye contact. Sometimes, the correct handshake will make or break a deal for you. Imagine if you are running your own business and you provide a quote for service. Your competitor comes in with the exact same quote. The only difference? You were able to inject a feeling of trust through your persona, including a firm and confident handshake. As we already know, people buy from people they know, like, and trust. So, which company do you think your client will go with? When comparing apples to apples, little things make the difference.

It is noteworthy to mention that it is acceptable for women to decline a handshake in a social setting or for men not to reach for women's hands. In a business setting, women should be prepared to shake hands with anyone present.

EYE CONTACT & SMILING

After my arrival, I recall telling Mom that, unlike in Uzbekistan, people in this country looked into my eyes and smiled even if they didn't know me. Having a stranger greet me or even wave their hand felt awkward. My discomfort faded slowly, and I started to mimic American greeting practices. After more than five years, when I first traveled back to Uzbekistan, I felt awkward when people didn't greet, smile, or wave at me if they didn't know me.

Analyzing Uzbek behavior and comparing it to my new American reality, I can say that I now prefer this friendlier approach. If you think about it, we don't have to know someone personally just to brighten up their day. We should be willing to do this to any person we encounter.

I guess that's what they mean when they say, "America has a tendency to grow on you."

HOSTING/ATTENDING PARTIES

Social tendencies are also very different in my country of origin. In Uzbekistan, houseguests are perceived as rude if they begin eating food as soon as it has been served. According to Uzbek cultural norms, guests first decline the food, and hosts insist they take it. The same holds true for alcoholic beverages. When guests begin to leave, Uzbek hosts encourage them to stay a tad longer—always adhering to an old saying: "The guest is as honored as your father."

In the United States, things are quite different. Guests are expected to eat as much as they like, and seconds are not uncommon. Also, when entering a house, there is no consistent rule about removing shoes, and it's best to just ask your host what you should do.

You can, of course, imagine my surprise the first time I encountered a buffet, unheard of in Uzbekistan at the time. Now, they are common even in Uzbekistan—the West creeping slowly into the East.

Where is the best place to meet people from your home country, you may ask? Introductions worked best for me, as well as attending gatherings, especially those that attract larger crowds, such as celebrating a holiday specific to your country. You may also have luck meeting like-minded people in social media groups and places of worship, attending country-specific activities, and being a part of community centers.

IMPROMPTU VISITS & STAYING IN TOUCH

Another thing I have always loved about my home culture is the option to check up on friends. In Uzbekistan, it is not uncommon to drop in on someone unannounced and then be hosted as you expected. These impromptu gatherings do much to create a sense of commmunity. However, after fifteen years in the United States, my perception has shifted slightly, and I can recognize how these get-togethers might be burdensome.

Before visiting a friend or a neighbor in the U.S., you should always call first to ensure they can see you. Be considerate of their time and know that you should not stay too long.

In the United States, everyone is so busy, and impromptu visits are unusual. Many people I know finish an eight-hour shift at their full-time job, then shuffle off immediately to a shift at their part-time job. After working twelve hours (or more), they eat, sleep, and repeat the cycle. Consequently, relationships are often sacrificed for money. This was made clear to me back in 2005 when my brother passed away. Prior to his death, I would rush our phone calls—well aware of how much I was being charged for the long-distance communications. Looking back, I would do almost anything to disregard the cost and enjoy talking to my brother when I still had the chance.

GEOGRAPHY & PERCEPTION

I was also surprised to realize how I was perceived in the United States. Not a lot of Americans even know where Uzbekistan is. It's not completely surprising since only about twenty-five percent of American 8th graders have proficient knowledge in geography as it is a subject that is not given much focus and not even required in most states. I can't blame them. That said, Uzbekistan is located in Central Asia, and we consider ourselves Asian. However, we are still perceived as Russians because our nation was part of the USSR several decades earlier. In practical terms, this irritating misapprehension means that Uzbeks cannot apply for benefits available to minority groups—even though our nation of 33+ million has only 100,000 expatriates living in the United States.

FIREARMS

The right to bear arms is seen as enshrined in the Second Amendment of the U.S. Constitution. This means people can possess and, in some cases, carry guns. Sadly, history is full of instances where a dictator was able to retain power over an unarmed nation by brutally suppressing the opposition using an army. The Founding Fathers most likely included it to stop possible government abuse of control over the people and prevent the need for the U.S. to have a professional army.

If you come from a country that forbids civilian firearm possession, owning a gun may interest you. If that is the case, try out a shooting range. The best way to find it is by searching online. Each shooting range may have slightly different rules. The staff, in most cases, will give you the basics of firearm handling, and some may require you to sit through a short orientation class.

The right to own or carry a firearm is state-specific. Some states have more stringent requirements than others. For example, Maryland and California don't allow open carry, and concealed carry permits can be obtained only under strict conditions. In states like Utah, Kentucky, and Vermont, one can open carry without a license. Make sure you know the laws of your state before purchasing or carrying a firearm.

If you find yourself in an argument, keep in mind that the person could be armed. There are plenty of cases where an armed person ended somebody's life during a heated argument that went out of control. It's not the case in Uzbekistan because firearms ownership is forbidden, so most people don't own firearms. It's not allowed. The worst cases are usually stabbings, where one's chances of survival are much higher. Suppose you find yourself in a situation that is getting heated: try to resolve it peacefully. If it's impossible, take your dispute to the courts, but don't try to "fix it" right there and then. The risk is too significant, and it's simply not worth it.

I don't want you to think this is the Wild West. It's not. In fact, most incidents do not involve firearms. I want you to be mindful, as the saying goes, better safe than sorry.

The same goes for road rage situations. Don't get wound up if someone cuts you off on the road. The consequences may be dire.

After my arrival, a crying man on the news attracted my attention. I started to listen to his story. Apparently, he was involved in a road rage incident with another driver, who then pulled out a gun and shot at him. The bullet missed him, but it hit and killed his daughter sitting in the back seat. His cry and his message were so painful that, to date, it shakes me whenever I recall the memory.

I heard the following technique on the radio, which seems to work well should I feel my anxiety rising due to someone else's reckless driving:

Imagine allowing the other person to drive recklessly, literally giving them permission to do so. Say to yourself, "I allow you to be an idiot and drive stupidly (e.g., fast/slow/ cut off/honk, etc.)." By permitting them to do so, you put yourself back in control and "let" the other guy act foolishly.

BRIBERY & CORRUPTION

Some immigrants come from cultures where bribery is not only accepted but, in many cases, almost necessary. In the United States, this is not the case. Here, attempting to bribe a police officer is a punishable crime.

That is not to say that bribery doesn't exist in the U.S. Unfortunately, there are bad people everywhere. The main difference is that the law punishes bribery with much more seriousness, making it rarer and more regulated than in other parts of the world.

Don't try it. The potential for trouble far outweighs the likelihood of gain.

The only bribery you can get away with, that is socially acceptable, is so-called "ethical bribing." This term is common in the business world. For example, you could provide an incentive and/or quick win to someone who signs up for your marketing mailing list.

DOES SIZE REALLY MATTER?

When I first arrived, I couldn't help noticing that items/ things were oversized/bigger in the States compared to Uzbekistan. It's nothing major, just something to be aware of. The examples range from chewing gum and food por- tions and drinks served at restaurants to cars, houses, etc.

DATING

You may also find dating quite different in the U.S. In Uzbekistan, we were raised with a motto: "If you can't afford to pay for your date's dinner, don't invite her to dine with you." That's why it's customary for men to pay for a night out with their date. This is not necessarily the case in the U.S. Imagine my surprised face when the first date offered to split the bill after dinner.

Where can you meet your soulmate in the U.S.? The answer is: anywhere – during sightseeing, online dating and apps, at work, in community or social group events (e.g., Latin/ballroom dance sessions, cooking classes, yoga class, poetry reading, etc.), clubs, movies, bars, and the list goes on. The important thing is to take action, don't get too tangled up in your head because fear will freeze you, and you may never get another chance to approach that person again.

Recall the golden rule of any salesperson: The worst thing that can happen is you get a no, which is harmless by nature. But what if the answer is yes?!

I want to add one more point: Don't rush the events once the conversation is flowing. In my experience, girls here like it when guys respect their personal space. Having said that, I am only speaking from a guy's perspective. Also, I don't think that many will argue that intelligence, sense of humor, and success are appreciated in any culture, for any gender—more reasons for you to work on yourself and your personal development.

DRESS CODE

Or perhaps I should say the absence of a dress code. Back home, we would work hard to create a successful image. In the States, you will notice that people don't care as much about how you are dressed. In many situations, comfort here comes first—though exceptions certainly exist.

Finding a shirt, matching the top with the bottom, then the bottom with the belt, then the belt with the socks, the socks with the shoes, etc., requires a lot of decision-making power. And if you do it every single day, or multiple times a day, you are spending a ton of energy just on how you look. Not to mention doing up one's hair, shaving, makeup, etc., unless you work in an industry that requires you to constantly look made up.

Did you know that many influential and successful people actually own the same or similar clothing? This way they have one less decision to take. Instead, they preserve this energy to resolve bigger concerns at hand, which can actually create a difference.

I have seen a lot of successful and affluent people dressing comfortably, and most importantly, simply. Have you noticed that Steve Jobs would always dress in the same black turtleneck shirt, jeans, and sneakers?

WRITING STYLE

Styles of writing may also vary considerably from culture to culture. For example, in Uzbekistan, writers format their arguments circularly, allowing readers to reach their own conclusions.

In the United States, persuasive writing is much more to the point. A statement is made in the opening paragraph and then supported throughout the text. Knowing how to write and communicate effectively can be very helpful throughout your career and personal growth. Fine writing is a stepping stone to success, especially for immigrants whose first language is not English.

PATIENCE & RESPECT

One of the things that positively surprised me was how respectful Americans are toward others. This can be observed in small things such as waiting patiently in line or even stopping at a stop sign.

Unfortunately, in my home country, I have noticed people in positions of power or the rich/elite taking advantage of situations without showing respect toward the "little guy".

U.S. HOLIDAYS

Most federal agencies will be closed on official holidays. Should the holiday fall on a Saturday, it's observed on the preceding Friday. Should it fall on Sunday, it will be observed the following Monday.

Observation of these holidays is not required for non-government employers. It's entirely up to your employer whether to observe the holiday. Sometimes employers pay time and a half to work on one of these days to encourage employee coverage. Refer to your employment terms for more info.

Below is the list of Federal Holidays.

1. New Year's Day - January 1st
2. Martin Luther King, Jr (MLK) Day - 3rd Monday in January
3. Presidents' Day - 3rd Monday in February
4. Memorial Day - Last Monday in May
5. Independence Day - July 4th
6. Labor Day - 1st Monday in September
7. Columbus Day - 2nd Monday in October
8. Veterans Day - November 11th
9. Thanksgiving Day - 4th Thursday in November
10. Christmas Day - December 25th

WEATHER

America is so blessed with having a diverse climate. If you prefer one or the other season, or a combination, in most cases, you can find a state that will suit you.

For example, you can experience all four seasons in New York City, Baltimore, and Denver while the air is humid. In Denver, summers are hot, and winters are very cold and snowy. In Florida, the weather is mostly hot and humid, and in Arizona, it's very hot and dry. In Alaska, you will experience the coldest weather in the States. In Puerto Rico, you will feel like you are in the tropics.

If you are unsure, do a search before you arrive, and of course, pack your clothes accordingly. And if you get an opportunity to travel throughout the States, do so as you can experience not only the weather firsthand but also the people, cuisine, and culture.

Here are the dates for the start of each season:

- Spring: March 20
- Summer: June 21
- Fall: September 23.
- Winter: December 21

CICADAS

I still find these bugs exotic. At first, they seemed very bizarre and somewhat disturbing, a mixture of a bug with a dragonfly.

They emerge from underground every thirteen or seventeen years, primarily during May and June. Depending upon your state, you may see them as often as every year. This is because they don't all come out at once. There are different groups of cicadas, and each emerges in different years. Be prepared to use your windshield wipers more often and have them fully colonize your trees once they arrive.

I am highlighting cicadas because I have experienced them firsthand in Maryland. Cicadas are isolated to specific parts of the U.S.

The U.S., however, has many critters in various places that require attention. For example, in some regions, you may need to watch for bears, rattlesnakes, or coyotes.

MAGIC IS IN THE AIR

Especially in the beginning, it appeared that I had moved into a land of magic from the fairytales: the squirrels, foxes, deer in the backyard, eagles soaring in the blue sky, beautiful scenery including lush forests, clean air, water, and fireflies lighting up the night.

Despite all these years, these things still give me joy and pleasure when I lay my eyes upon them.

Congratulations on finishing Chapter 4!

Use the following questions to help you reflect on the chapter you just read.

1. Name 3 things common in your country but not in the U.S.

2. What's your English proficiency rating on a scale of 1 to 10? What's your next step?

3. What's your stance on the controversial issue of gun ownership in the U.S.? Do you currently possess a firearm?

Your progress so far   31%

4/13

CHAPTER 5

RELIGION

Let me start by saying that I respect all peaceful religions and those who practice them. As I write this very sentence on our family trip back from Sarasota, FL, my father, Najmiddin Shukurov, is praying in the seat next to me.

My respect extends to those who choose not to practice any religion so long as the person possesses strong morals and ethics. What upsets me is when a person tries to push their belief system, or lack thereof, on another party or chooses to bring harm to themselves or others.

In this chapter, we will discuss how I see religion and what separates religious practice in the U.S. from what I witnessed in Uzbekistan.

Now, let me take you back in time. After the Bolsheviks overturned the Russian Empire, Uzbekistan fell under the control of the Union of Soviet Socialist Republics (U.S.S.R.) and stayed as such until the Soviet collapse in 1991.

The U.S.S.R. controlled vast territory comprising different nations, each with its own traditions, religions, belief systems, and politics. The Soviets realized that faith and politics were two main things that could ignite unrest.

The U.S.S.R. operated under a single, unopposed Soviet ideology. This left only religion as a possible source of contention among the Soviet republics. Instead of pushing a singular faith as the "true religion," the U.S.S.R outlawed all faiths.

Although Uzbekistan is and has been a predominantly Muslim country, growing up, I don't recall anyone in our circle practicing religion. People wouldn't even talk about it.

Once Uzbekistan gained its independence, religious practice was once again permitted. In a few short years, I witnessed some of my countrymen moving far right with religion after being brainwashed by so-called "true" religious followers. Unfortunately, some became extreme and even executed terror attacks against our people.

In my opinion, the cause of such behavior was ignorance and the inability to separate true good from radical ideology, attributable in part to the fact that we weren't educated about religion in school or growing up. The Uzbek government realized it and cracked down on religious extremism.

Why am I telling you this? As we already know, anything over healthy moderation becomes toxic. Examples include extreme dieting and working out. Be mindful of who you let whisper in your ears day in and day out, and pay attention to what content you consume.

In the U.S., your right to practice or not practice religion is protected by law. In fact, it's spelled out in the First Amendment of the Constitution.

I find people here are very tolerant when it comes to religion. Although the United States remains a predominantly Christian nation, in many small cities, you can easily find several churches, a synagogue, a mosque, and probably other places of worship too. Often these sites are even situated on the same streets.

I have observed some immigrants shift to the far right after arriving in the States, overwhelmed with the freedom to practice, unable to filter out good from bad. Unfortunately, there are multitudes of so-called "righteous religious leaders," especially on the internet. Stay alert. It's easy to find yourself heading down a rabbit hole from which you may be unable to return.

How can you separate good from the bad? By asking yourself whether your actions or inaction would cause harm to someone else or yourself. If the answer is yes, you are likely on the wrong path.

Although we all come from different parts of the world with our beliefs, skin tones, traditions, and cultures, we all represent one human nation. We all have a beating heart, and none are excused from feeling pain and suffering.

The following saying, which I read in an Airbnb in Montreal, resonated with me: "One's freedom ends where another's begins."

I also believe in the separation of church and state. I think one should not get involved with the affairs of the other.

Congratulations on finishing Chapter 5!

Use the following questions to help you reflect on the chapter you just read.

1. Would you consider religion a significant factor in migrating to the USA?

2. How does embracing diverse religions in the USA foster a sense of connection and community for you?

3. How does your religion influence your immigrant experience in the USA? Is it a barrier or a chance to enhance your faith while connecting with Americans? How do you navigate this aspect of your identity while pursuing your American Dream?

Your progress so far   38%

5/13

CHAPTER 6
THE POWER OF LANGUAGE

By the end of this chapter, you will learn the power and possibilities that come with learning the language of the land and methods to improve the learning process, including the federal aid program to accelerate language learning.

Immigrants who don't speak English put themselves at an enormous disadvantage. Though very difficult to master, fluency in English opens a new world of opportunities. Not speaking the language closes the door to them.

I have known many doctors, lawyers, and engineers from post-Soviet countries who had no choice but to work in trucking, construction, or other blue-collar jobs because they failed to become fluent in English.

Let's face it, there are always excuses should we look for them: "If I had more time," "If the bills were not so high," "If I had more energy," etc. Indeed, these rationalizations may seem valid on the surface. Life is challenging enough without added complications, yet the benefits of overcoming these hurdles are enormous. When a doctor from a foreign country finally masters a language, passes the board examinations exam, and becomes a doctor in the

United States, their life will forever change positively. As Stephen R. Covey, author of *The 7 Habits of Highly Effective People*, said: "Happiness--in part at least--is the fruit of the desire and ability to sacrifice what we want now for what we want eventually."

After all, did you come to the U.S. just to throw away all those years of training and experience?

Identify what is holding you back from learning English. Then work harder on it until you master it. Since repetition leads to perfection, the more you work on it, the better you will become at it. If it's the grammar, consider hiring a tutor (you can even engage one from your country and opt in for weekly virtual classes). If it's the vocabulary, then set a goal of learning X number of words a day, and use various techniques such as applying sticky notes to objects so you can see their translation every time you use that particular object. If it's the pronunciation, listen to English music and movies and pay closer attention to how locals pronounce certain words. You get the gist.

As immigrants, we know that most of us may have a strong accent, our vocabulary could be relatively poor, and/or our grammar skills may not be perfect. Instinctually, we gravitate toward using our native tongue whenever possible. This is fine—but it should not be at the expense of learning English. The more we speak the language, the faster we learn it. Practice at every opportunity available, and get into the habit of speaking despite possible mistakes.

Fear of being laughed at kept me back initially. Once I overcame it, I started making substantial progress in my language-learning skills. How did I do it? I firmly committed to speaking the language at every opportunity, despite my mistakes.

You will find most Americans will be patient and even encouraging. In my experience, they generally perceive it as flattering when we try.

After being in this country for seventeen years and running various successful businesses, my office staff still corrects my English. Just today, I told my friend's wife to peek her nose into my business partner's office to see if he is busy, yet instead of peek (/pēk/), I pronounced it pick (/pik/). Basically, it came out as if I told her to literally "pick her nose." You can probably imagine how the entire office burst into laughter. But instead of getting offended, I encourage those around me to correct my mistakes whenever possible. Otherwise, how will I know that I am making a mistake?

Committing to learning the language and taking action are the most important things. The rest will come with practice. Do yourself and me a favor, my friend, put this book aside and go in front of the mirror. Look in the eyes of the person you see there and promise the following two things: (1) From now on, you will learn three new words each day, from Monday to Friday, and rehearse them all on Saturday. That is fifteen new words a week, 780 new words a year. (2) Going forward, you will communicate in English with every American you interact with without asking your friends/relatives/kids to translate for you, even if you must use an app such as Google Translate. Evaluate your progress after following this practice for the next three months and readjust your strategy based on that progress.

Listening to English music, podcasts, and audiobooks and watching television can also increase your vocabulary and improve your learning efforts. Don't hold yourself back. Don't be afraid—speak up!

One might think they can get by in the U.S. without learning English. That it's not an absolute necessity due to the diversity and accommodations available in the country. And, to some extent, they would be right, to an extent. But there is so much s/he misses out on when s/he doesn't speak the primary language of a country.

Let's say you need to file simple immigration documentation. By knowing English, you may be able to take care of it yourself and save not only on the attorney's fees but also your time and energy associated with back and forth. Even if money isn't an issue, you're still missing out on the rich cultural and intellectual experience of learning a language. Additionally, learning languages even helps improve attention capabilities[7] and possibly delays the onset of Alzheimer's[8].

Now, maybe you do desire to learn English, but money is an issue, perhaps time as well. The good news is that there are many free resources for learning languages, especially for beginners (but also for all levels):

---

[7] "How learning a new language helps brain development." https://www.whitbyschool.org/passionforlearning/learning-a-new-language-helps-brain-development. Accessed 4 Mar. 2022.

[8] "Bilingualism as a strategy to delay the onset of Alzheimer's disease." 19 Oct. 2017, https://www.ncbi.nlm.nih.gov/pmc/articles/PMC5656355/. Accessed 4 Mar. 2022.

- USA Learns (*www.usalearns.org*)
- Duolingo (*www.duolingo.com*)
- FluentU (*www.fluentu.com*)
- LearnEnglish (*www.learnenglish.de*)
- Grammarly (*www.grammarly.com*)
- Google Translate (*www.translate.google.com*)

And most language-learning tools these days emphasize that the amount of time you spend on learning is less important than the *consistency* with which you practice. This means that studying for six hours each weekend won't be as effective as practicing daily for thirty minutes .

Making language learning a small part of your daily routine is the key to success. Eventually, you'll need to move on to spend more time with the language, but at that point, you'll start being able to "immerse" rather than just "study." That is, instead of setting aside an hour to study, you can now begin to do in English something you have been doing every day in your native language. Perhaps you watch the news every afternoon; now try watching it in English (maybe starting with subtitles and progressing over time).

Another example is taking classes at a local community college or library (many libraries offer free English-learning classes as well) in the U.S. can be a great way to get out more and meet other people in similar situations. Not only can this blunt the impact of culture shock, it can also help speed up your transition.

If you are interested in pursuing college in the United States, you should know that you can apply for financial aid through the Federal Student Aid program.

The process is fairly simple and easy to complete:

- Create an online account at *www.studentaid.gov*.
- Fill out the FAFSA form.
- Wait for approval and/or further instructions.

Student counseling centers at the college you are interested in should be able to point you in the right direction.

Exploring English as a way to integrate doesn't mean losing your native language. Some immigrants stop using their own language altogether, especially around their children, as they want them to grow up fully American. This is understandable considering some of the harsh treatment immigrants receive for being different in the U.S. Having said that, times are changing. Diversity is embraced increasingly, and being multilingual is now often recognized as an advantage.

Needless to say that writing is also a vital element of adjusting to the English language. How you write says a lot about you. One reason I can deliver this book to you is that I taught myself how to write.

Let's bring up another realistic scenario that can happen to either of us: You are disputing a contractual breach with your client/employer/apartment complex/etc. How well you can elaborate on your points in writing and describe your position may influence how much bargaining power you get in return.

And let's not forget that reading well-written content from you is generally more pleasing to the other party.

I recognize writing as an Achilles heel for myself and make adjustments to compensate. For example, a paid subscription to Grammarly (*www.grammarly.com*) helps me iron out my writing with relative ease. In your current stage of life, proper writing may not yet be too important. However, as you advance through life, the importance of writing will most likely increase. Don't be embarrassed to ask for help or even use freelancers while you sharpen your own writing skills.

I find that learning a language is an infinite game without an end, especially for an immigrant. There is no winning or losing, only continuous forward motion.

READING

Not only is reading vital to master a language, it's also highly effective for personal growth and skill acquisition. The benefits that come from reading are genuinely impressive.

Our world today is more connected than ever before. There are countless streaming services, social media and news channels, search engines, and more. They are all designed to keep us in front of the screen hour after hour. These billion-dollar companies use persuasive design techniques[9] with the goal of "feeding" us exactly what we want.

---

[9] "Tech companies use "persuasive design" to get us hooked - Vox." 8 Aug. 2018, https://www.vox.com/2018/8/8/17664580/persuasive-technology-psychology. Accessed 4 Mar. 2022.

The longer they keep us tuned in, the more popularity they gain while fattening their wallets.

In this world full of noise, it's easy to lose track of time by trying to stay connected. I have done it myself over and over. Disconnecting is what we need.

One of the best methods to disconnect is by reading. Not only can it help you unplug for a bit, but it also carries an endless list of benefits. Also, remember that readers have higher-paying jobs, better memories, and improved concentration, placing a high value on the practice. I can't emphasize the importance of reading enough and want to encourage you to make it part of your daily routine.

Below, you will find some tips from Jim Kwik's *Limitless: Upgrade Your Brain, Learn Anything Faster, and Unlock Your Exceptional Life:*

"Baby steps" technique: Let's face it, most of us are good at procrastination. Avoid it by taking small steps. For example, if your goal is to read a book, start with five pages and go from there.

Don't use subvocalization: Apparently, most of us read two hundred words per minute. Pronouncing each word in your head as you read slows you down simply because you can read only as fast as you talk. Instead, try counting aloud when you read (1,2,3, etc.) as you go down the page. It's not easy, especially initially, yet it will train your mind to subvocalize less.

With practice and in due time, reading will become easier. The goal is to train yourself so that reading feels more like watching a movie than hearing a speech.

Use a pacer: Our eyes are wired to track a moving object. Try sliding your finger down the page as you read. This simple technique alone can increase your reading speed by 25% to a whopping 100%.

Be consistent: As with everything, practice and regularity are key—schedule at least thirty minutes of reading time every day. As they say, perfect practice makes perfect!

Just for a second, imagine the opposite. Let's swap out your home country with the United States. Your country is the world leader, and countless immigrants are moving into your country to pursue a better life.

As a native, wouldn't it be easier to welcome, connect with, and help integrate a newcomer who speaks or is learning to speak your language?

For the same reasons, it's imperative to learn English when you decide to immigrate to the United States. English is the language of the land. Communicating with Americans clearly will undoubtedly propel you to new heights, some you may not have even imagined.

Congratulations on finishing Chapter 6!

Use the following questions to help you reflect on the chapter you just read.

1. How does limited English proficiency complicate your life as an immigrant in the USA?

2. Have you encountered challenges or unfair treatment due to language differences with Americans? How did you manage those situations?

3. Describe how learning American English has aided your personal growth and connections.

Your progress so far   46%

6/13

CHAPTER 7
IMMIGRATING WITH CHILDREN

In this chapter, we will talk about immigrating to the U.S. with kids, regardless of whether you are a single parent or a couple. Its content is designed to provide valuable information regarding enrolling your children in school and is broken down into digestible smaller steps to ease and simplify the otherwise cumbersome process. You will also learn about after-school activities and Child Protective Services (CPS).

Moving with children is very difficult. Leaving everything and everyone you know and immigrating to a new county for good is mind-boggling for an adult, let alone a child. Think how much easier it would be if one parent immigrated a little earlier, secured housing, got acclimated, found a job, and made friends, especially those with kids. This would undoubtedly make the transition and the culture shock for the children a little smoother.

That said, there is no right or wrong way of doing it. Many before you have moved successfully to the States with their families , and many will do it after you. Thus, each decision must be taken by weighing the pros and cons and considering your family's unique situation.

NEIGHBORHOOD

Regardless of buying or renting, be certain you make a conscious choice about the neighborhood and school district. Not only should you like the area but you should also feel safe there. For example, some communities vary drastically in Baltimore from block to block. It's not a bad idea to visit the preselected neighborhood at various times, especially in the evenings as everyone is returning from work or school, and observe/learn about the neighborhood and its residents.

Did you notice any suspicious behavior/activity? Drugs? Prostitution? Lawlessness? Would you be comfortable having your kids play in that community? What if they were to walk to the school? Would you feel safe about it?

On top of the price, also consider other amenities such as proximity to shopping, recreational areas, kids' playgrounds, etc. If you don't drive, evaluate the distance from your to-be home to your workplace/school, the nearest grocery store, pharmacy, public transportation, medical facilities, etc.

Search the web for information on crime, property values, schools, services, etc. Various websites will show different data on the neighborhoods, breaking it down by crime statistics, ethnicity, income, age, school districts, renters vs. homeowners, etc.

Further, relocating overall after settling is not easy and can be stressful. People generally don't relocate until they experience a significant change in circumstances, such as family expansion, relocation due to work, purchasing a house vs. renting, etc. If your circumstances change, do your due diligence before moving into a particular house.

Moving into a neighborhood where your friends and family members are already living may make your adaptation easier, especially if they have settled in the U.S. before you. They usually are a good source of knowledge and connections, and can help with documentation to get started.

Before purchasing my first house, my main requirement was the school district. I had the option to purchase a bigger and newer house in a neighborhood where I, as an adult, would feel okay, but the schools had poor ratings, or to put an offer in on a smaller, run-down house that needed quite a bit of work but with good schools.

You guessed right: I ended up purchasing the run-down house. At that very moment, when my daughters weren't born yet, the decision may have seemed a little unwise. However, after ten years, I can confirm that my intuition didn't let me down. Not only did my children get to attend better schools, but property values appreciated a lot more compared to the less desirable neighborhoods where I could have gotten a bigger house for my buck over time as folks tend to stay longer in neighborhoods with better schools.

CHILDCARE

In Uzbekistan, childcare services are relatively inexpensive. Uzbeks also tend to have a large support group, and asking someone to watch over your babies isn't such a big deal.

In America, though, things are different. Even if you are lucky to have a large circle of friends and family in the States, you will find that people here are always busy and may not have time to watch after your children at a moment's notice. Besides, there are only so many times you can ask one for a favor, right?

Childcare services and babysitters in the States are costly. It's partly due to the expensive labor, intensive regulations, and compliance. Finding someone from your community to babysit your children may be the most economical option for you.

Based on your economic circumstances, you may also qualify for childcare financial assistance, aka vouchers/certificates/subsidies. States get funding from the government to help provide childcare assistance for low-income families. You may learn more about programs, including tax credits and other support, at the following website: *www.childcare.gov/consumer-education/get-help-paying-for-child-care*.

Follow this link to find out more about specific programs and other resources, including the children's health insurance program (CHIP) and the supplemental nutrition assistance program (SNAP) offered by your state: *www.childcare.gov/state-resources-home*.

Applying for federal subsidies and other assistance programs may hurt your case when applying for citizenship. If unsure, consult with a legal professional about your particular circumstances.

SCHOOLS & HIGHER EDUCATION

The U.S. provides free education from kindergarten through grade 12 for all students.

Unfortunately, in America, not every public school is great. Private schools usually tend to be much better, but they are expensive. GreatSchools (*www.greatschools.org*) is an excellent resource for researching the schools in your school district.

School is compulsory throughout the U.S. for children ages 5 to 16-18 (the age at which one can discontinue their schooling varies). Therefore, enroll your child/ren into school as soon as possible. Failure to do so may even negatively affect your parenting rights, especially if you are undergoing a divorce. The U.S. system pays close attention to general education.

The following is the required paperwork to enroll your child in school. The requirements may vary based on your school.

- Registration forms provided by the school.

- Birth certificate for each child.

- Proof of residency, e.g., deed or lease.

- Most recent copies of documents such as a bank statement, telephone bill, or electric bill, in your name and usually dated within the past sixty days.

- English as a Second Language (ESL) Test. ESL classes are taken for children over 1st grade. If your child is in kindergarten or younger, then in most cases, this won't apply to you. The school will schedule the test to assess the child's English-language knowledge. Some parents may worry that the lack of English may place their child in a lower grade than their counterparts. Don't panic, the ESL classes are usually scheduled during school hours and don't affect your child's grade placement. Kids are like sponges, they pick up the language quicker than adults. I am confident that your child will be speaking English fluently and may start helping you out with translations in no time. I have seen this happen over and over again.

- Medical examinations confirming your child's fitness for school include immunization records, dental records, overall health assessment, etc.

- If applicable, proof of prior school experience. This documentation must be obtained from your child's school before immigrating to the states. It will indicate completed grades, credits received, etc.

- Registering parents' photo ID.

Most schools are organized the following way:

1. Elementary/Primary School - Kindergarten and Grades 1 to 5 or 1 to 6. Ages 5 to 11.

2. Junior/Middle School - Grades 6 to 8, 7 to 8, or 7 to 9. Ages 11 to 14.

3. Secondary/High School - Grades 9 to 12 or 10 to 12. Ages 14 to 18, and sometimes up to 21.

4. Postsecondary/Higher Education - Community colleges, Two or four-year colleges, universities, trade schools. Ages, all eligible adults.

Many schools offer free buses to pick up and drop off a student. Optionally they can walk or ride a bike or parents can drive the kids.

The school year typically runs from August or September until May or June, though many schools are on a year-round schedule. Some schools offer free or low-cost meals. The public school typically provides books; parents usually buy the kids' school supplies (backpacks, paper, pencils, etc.)

In the States, all students have the right to get a free education whether or not they have a disability. If you think your child is being bullied, visit the following website to learn how to identify it and help your child to overcome it: *www.stopbullying.gov.*

Also contact the school guidance counselor who will become an advocate on behalf of your child and help your child navigate the difficulties.

Should you need to communicate with your child's teacher, you can schedule a meeting in school or talk via phone, email, and sometimes text message. Teachers will most likely have a private web page or social media account on which they keep the class's photos and activities so students and parents can stay in the know.

After high school, adults can continue their education. The following are higher education degrees types, where they can be obtained, and how long, in general, they take to achieve:

- Certificate - community college/trade school - six months to two years.
- Associate's - community college - two years.
- Bachelor's - four-year college or university - four years.
- Master's - university - two years.

- Doctorate - university - two to eight years.
- Professional - specialized school - two to five years.

A university or college degree can get very expensive, especially for out-of-state or out-of-country residents. Luckily, the U.S. provides financial aid to students to help pay for their expenses, such as tuition, fees, book supplies, and transportation.

Primarily, there are three types of federal aid a student can qualify for:

1. Grants don't have to be paid back.
2. Work-study allows you to earn money by working while at school.
3. Loans must be repaid with interest.

Be sure to research any loan you are considering in terms of interest rates, repayment plans, and other terms.

SPORTS, ACTIVITIES, & RECREATION

Growing up in Uzbekistan, after school, I would mostly play outside in the neighborhood with my friends and return home closer to dinner. Back then, we didn't have cell phones and paid courses, and after-school activities weren't popular. I would simply let my parents know which friends I was going to hang out with. If I was needed, they would either call one of my friend's landline home phones or come looking for me in that particular neighborhood. We lived by the principle that it takes a village to raise a child.

Why am I telling you this? Because in America, things are slightly different. My daughters, ages 9 and 6, return home after school. Since there aren't many kids of their age in our neighborhood, we (the parents) try to keep them busy with various activities.

Signing up for your local Y (aka YMCA), local gym/community center, may not be a bad idea. You will pay one fixed monthly fee, and in return, you will have access to a gym and pool, limited-time daycare to take care of your children, child-specific classes and activities. The Ys also offers financial assistance and income-based memberships. More can be found on this website: *www.ymcagbw.org/membership/financialassistance*.

Local libraries are also great places to spend time with kids. They are a great knowledge resource, don't cost money to sign up, and on top of books and movies to borrow, they may have theme-based activities to keep the kids engaged and learning. Besides, the earlier you start developing reading habits in your kids, the better it is for them.

Depending on your area, you may have outdoor activities such as parks, hiking, biking, etc. If there is an amusement or theme park nearby, inquiring about the yearly passes may not be a bad idea.

Optionally, consider signing up your children based on their experience in private classes such as tennis, piano, drawing, music, self-defense, summer camps, etc. Ask your community members and google what's close to you. The additional classes may get costly. That is why I recommend signing up your child for activities s/he likes, and you have time to take them to.

Sports, in general, are essential for America and Americans. Popular sports include American football, baseball, basketball, and soccer. If your child is good at sports, then they may even be able to get into a college. Of course, sports performance is unlikely to be the single determining factor for getting into a college, but it's not totally impossible if your child is a top athlete.

CHILD PROTECTIVE SERVICES (CPS)

While growing up, I was spanked two times in my butt by my dad. Looking back now, I can tell you that those spanks were very well deserved! It's not uncommon to see a parent smacking a child to "teach them a lesson" in many other countries.

According to LawInfo, spanking is legal in many states, whereas abuse (choking, sexual abuse, providing a child with illegal drugs, burning) is unlawful. If a parent is accused, a judge or jury would need to decide based on the state's law. Follow this link to learn more differences between spanking and abuse: *www.lawinfo.com/resources/criminal-defense/when-does-discipline-become-abuse.html.*

We know children can be manipulative when attempting to "blackmail" their parents. Having a one-on-one heart-to-heart conversation with a child helps in these situations. Let your child understand that if they falsely report abuse, even in a playful-casual conversation with their teacher or nanny/babysitters, this can lead to a full-blown investigation by authorities.

More information about Child Protective Services (CPS) and how to contact them can be found on this website: *www.childcare.gov/consumer-education/child-protective-services*.

Some children are more active than others. If your child is one of those and comes home with scratches and bruises all the time, then they will be asked about the source by a babysitter, school teacher, and/or nurse. If the answer is abuse, the case will be reported to authorities.

My friend Bob's oldest child is extremely active and constantly manages to get bruises and scratches. I still don't know where he gets all this energy from. At some point, the accidents happened back to back, and his teacher reported the case to the authorities, although the kid said he was only playing. An investigation was initiated. Eventually, the dust did settle down, and no actions were taken against the parents as they are indeed not the kind that abuse children. Regardless of the outcome, time and energy were wasted.

For most of us, there is nothing for us to worry about as our intentions are pure. Just be aware of the abovementioned things and keep giving your unlimited love and care to your offspring! The world desperately needs more good people!

Congratulations on finishing Chapter 7!

Use the following questions to help you reflect on the chapter you just read.

1. When choosing a place to live, what are the top 3 factors that matter most to you?

2. If you become a parent, what 3 career paths would you want your children to explore or pursue?

3. Have you or your children experienced bullying? How do you handle and mitigate these situations?

Your progress so far   54%

7/13

CHAPTER 8
BEST MINDSET & AMBITIONS

In this chapter, I will let you in on a secret that has helped me overcome obstacles and all challenges that life has thrown at me or I got myself into. I wish I had discovered it when I was still in my twenties. Pay close attention; once you learn this secret, you will become truly unstoppable.

The Oxford Languages definition of mindset is the established set of attitudes held by someone.

Essentially, it's how you view and experience the world around you.

Your mindset determines the things that you appreciate in life. It's easy to become oblivious to what is happening around you. To grow comfortable in the familiarity of routine and fail to grow or advance.

There was a stage in my life in which I was deep in the throes of an oblivious mindset. I had my wife, two adorable daughters, a single-family house with a two-car garage, two paid-off vehicles, and a growing business. I thought I had achieved the pinnacle of success. I became ignorant, stopped working on my personal growth altogether, and wasn't careful with the people I surrounded myself with. I preferred the company of people who would praise me and were always available to eat at my table.

For seven years, I felt invincible, all the while my house of cards began to crumble around me. I neglected my body, my mind, and my soul. And then, all at once, my lapses in judgment and neglect caught up with me. My wife left me, taking my daughters with her. My business began to fail. I even got pulled over for drinking and driving.

I began to feel the fatigue from stress on my body. Two of my three essential pillars—love/family and finances—were collapsing. I was fortunate that the last pillar, health, remained reasonably stable.

It started to occur to me that I had to do something to change the trajectory of my life and avoid the crash course. I just didn't know what exactly and where to start.

Most often, things that are free or easy get taken for granted. On the other hand, things that must be worked for and earned are usually valued much higher.

Inheriting wealth versus earning it for yourself can serve as a good example of this. If your parents leave you money, you may never really understand the risks and effort that went into accumulating the fortune in the first place.

Free things are not all bad, of course. There are many cases of people taking intergenerational wealth and increasing it. Similarly, second-generation immigrants often advance their family businesses to a whole new level.

However, if you start a business and experience its struggles personally, your feelings toward the fruit of that labor will be much different.

Are you familiar with the notion of a glass half full or half empty? It's supposed to be an indication of whether you are an optimist or pessimist. Positive folks, in general, tend to describe a glass as half full, whereas the pessimists see it as half empty.

Instead of asking why something is happening TO me, try asking why something is happening FOR me? This simple switch of prepositions can change the entire perspective on the given situation.

LIFE'S MAIN PILLARS & SELF-DEVELOPMENT

I believe that we all have three main pillars: (1) health, (2) love/family, and (3) finances. Dark thoughts can begin to cloud your mind when two of these pillars collapse. You may lose the will to live entirely when all three of them go. My situation was dire.

When life becomes bleak, it's crucial to identify the pillar that is easiest to fix and put all your effort into doing so. For example, if you are in financial ruin, look for work, even if it is part-time.

Around that time, I started having neck pain. After a few doctor's appointments and MRIs, it was diagnosed that my back muscles were weak, and I needed to strengthen them. I signed up for swimming classes and attended them pretty consistently. I started loving swimming. One day, the pool was closed for cleaning. Part of me was pleased for a chance to skip my workout, but a voice nagged at me to stay and exercise.

I did so, lifting some weights while listening to a podcast. It happened to be an episode where Hal Elrod (author of *The Miracle Morning*) was being interviewed. I listened to his life story as he explained who he was and, most importantly, HOW he achieved his success.

He said something that stuck with me, and it was along the following lines: You have achieved what you have today by being who you are. If you want more, you need to change and become more.

I also recall Hal quoting legendary Jim Rohn: "Your level of success will seldom exceed your level of personal development because success is something you attract by the person you become."

Thus began my journey toward personal development. Slowly, I started to notice that my surroundings began to change as I did.

The life that followed from this moment has been rich with joy and success. My health is better, my businesses are thriving, my ex-wife and I have repaired our relationship, and my children and I enjoy a close bond. I have even fallen in love! Was it easy? Absolutely not! Regardless of what situation you may find yourself in, continue moving forward and with an eye toward sustaining your pillars.

The moral of the story is to never stop working on yourself, never stop working on those that genuinely love you, and recognize what matters the most. Cut out the clutter and focus on what is truly important.

THE ESSENTIALS

Feed your body: Exercise at least every other day, ideally for thirty minutes or more. Get your heart rate up. Recognize you live in this body. If you mess it up, there will be no replacement. Another benefit of staying healthy is that when happiness and wealth come, you get to enjoy them in full health.

Feed your soul: Meditate and/or pray or find some other means to keep yourself grounded. I practice meditation five times a week. This skill will be extremely handy when winter (hard times) comes. And trust me, hard times always come; it's as inevitable as the change of seasons. Do the best you can to be prepared for it. As Jim Rohn said, "Don't wish it was easier, wish you were better. Don't wish for less problems, wish for more skills. Don't wish for less challenge, wish for more wisdom."

Feed your mind: Read and/or listen to (audio) books/podcasts/etc. Public libraries in the U.S. are free to the general public and a great resource for knowledge. They have not only books but also a wide variety of DVDs, computers with free internet access, newspapers, and other educational content, including language-learning programs such as Pimsleur and Rosetta Stone. You can also request specific items transferred from another facility if your local public library doesn't have them.

Libby (*www.libbyapp.com*) is a free application connected to your library card. It has a great variety of audiobooks, e-books, and magazines from your library. Library cards can be easily obtained by going into your local library or on their website.

Since a portion of your taxes already goes toward maintaining free public libraries, why not enjoy what you have already paid for?

Feed your ambitions: Visualize and/or use affirmations. Do this daily. Remove limiting beliefs. Don't be discouraged if the change doesn't happen immediately. Keep in mind that we all have been programmed with limiting beliefs for decades; thus, it will take years, if not more, to free us from those limiting beliefs and finally believe in ourselves and that we can change our destiny.

As Napoleon Hill said, "Whatever the mind can conceive and believe, the mind can achieve."

Visualization is the hardest for me. The key is not just to tell yourself what you want but to be able to feel it, smell it, and touch it. That's when it is most effective.

Give/Donate: Give your knowledge/wisdom, donate your time/labor, and/or money. You will feel good and start automatically attracting better things into your life. Trust me, the universe/God will give back multifold when your intentions are sincere.

As Melody Beattie said, "Gratitude turns what we have into enough." Be grateful for what you already have every single day. Your loved ones, your health, even the opportunity to have ever been born.

Pay attention to even the smallest things and be grateful for them. A place to park your car, running water, working electricity. Training yourself to be grateful is just like strengthening your body. It takes effort and repetition. Good thoughts attract good people, but the reverse is also true.

After some hard lessons, my goal now is to live my life by design rather than by default.

As mentioned above, don't be surprised or give up if changing your mindset takes longer than you expect.

Limiting beliefs are accumulated over a lifetime. They imprison our minds and bodies by telling us we are not enough and never will be. Replacing them with positive and encouraging thoughts may be a lengthy process which is very well worth it.

HABITS

Develop healthy habits. Habits are critical to creating a new, better version of yourself. As Will Durant said, "We are what we repeatedly do. Excellence, then, is not an act, but a habit."

Keep in mind that just as bad habits take time to form, they will also take time to break. Stick with the effort. The continued effort will eventually be rewarded when your healthy behaviors effectively replace bad alternatives.

In a study published in the *European Journal of Social Psychology* in 2010, a health psychology researcher at University College London, Phillippa Lally, and her research team explored how long it actually takes to form a habit.

They found that forming a new habit took anywhere from 18 to 254 days. According to the research, it usually takes more than two months for a new behavior to become automatic.

The good news? Once you form your first healthy habit, it usually leads to a second and then a third. James Clear, the author of *Atomic Habits*, calls this "habit stacking."

Allow me to share my habits with you, which I have cultivated over time and perform daily before anyone else is awake. They are listed in the same order as I execute them:

1. Wake up and drink water - Coffee or tea can come later, yet before anything else, hydration is vital.

2. We all know it's easy to get distracted by the outside world and its noise; therefore, I avoid using my phone despite the urge to check my emails or scan social media, at least until I finish all my morning rituals.

3. Work out - I use a seven-minute workout app. Not only does it get the blood flowing, but it also helps put me in a better mood.

4. Meditate - I used to use a guided meditation app. However, now I just enjoy silence for five to ten minutes. It helps me get grounded and calms my heart rate after the workout. The key is to keep your mind not thinking about anything. Keep it calm. Listen to your heartbeat or breathing if you must. After all, how often do we pause and appreciate our heart pumping blood and lungs breathing? Those are the things we take for granted.

5. Learn a language - Now that I am awake, and my mind is sharp, I sit down to learn a language. I am currently learning Spanish. I usually spend five to ten minutes on the Duolingo app right after the meditation without changing my sitting position.

6. Journaling - I record my thoughts, describe my schedule, and reflect on what I am grateful for. It usually happens in the evenings once the day is coming to its end so that I can write down the most important events of that day.

7. Read - I strive to read a book for at least twenty-five minutes daily. Growing up in the post-Soviet era, I felt that reading was undervalued, yet you get back way more than what you put into it. Authors share decades of experience and wisdom you can glimpse from the pages to avoid mistakes. How valuable is that! I enjoy the feeling of an actual hardcover book in my hands and always highlight meaningful passages to return to later.

8. Accountability - after completing all these steps, I take my phone and check in with my accountability partner. I report the tasks I was able to complete. If there is an unfinished task, I also let him know about it and when I intend to finish it. If life gets in the way and I can't finish the remaining task/s for that day, that's okay. No need to beat yourself up about it. The goal is to create the habit where you try to finish all your rituals and then check in.

   Finding the right accountability partner may be challenging and may require going through several partners. At least, that was the case for me. You will find as you grow and commit, not everyone will be able to keep up with your pace. This is technically good news for you because, generally, you are outgrowing your circle faster. It's okay to change accountability partners along the way.

As you may have noticed, habits #1 to #6 happen in the mornings. It usually takes me an hour to complete them all. I dedicate that very first hour of the day to myself. Some may think I am selfish and steal that hour from my loved ones. Yet if you think deeper about it, how many people can you help if you are sick, hungry, or poor? Now flip the coin, how many people are you capable of helping when you are rich, healthy, and in sound mind and soul?

That is precisely why I first take care of myself, nurture my body and mind, and ground my soul very first thing in the morning. This is what works for me. What works for me may not necessarily be the best fit for you. Feel free to try various strategies until you find your own routine.

Do this, and you will start noticing that even the days will become happier and more fulfilling. You have already accomplished many things and can now take on the day and whatever challenges it may bring. To make the time, consider waking up an hour earlier than usual. You may need to sleep earlier to compensate, but the benefits are worthwhile.

Instead of being reactive, you become proactive.

It's also worth mentioning that life will sometimes disrupt your habit-building efforts. Family, business/work, travel, and so on may interrupt your routines. Don't regret the time lost—just resume your efforts as soon as the opportunity arises. No need to make up for lost time or increase the intensity of your workouts, reading sessions, etc. Slow and steady wins the race.

TIME MANAGEMENT

Managing your time is important at work and outside of it. Striking a balance between work and life is essential.

For simplicity, you may wish to divide your day into three parts, allowing eight hours for work, eight hours of personal time, and eight hours of sleep.

I understand that, as immigrants who came here without anything, it's hard to just work eight hours, especially in the early days. I remember working sixteen hours every single day, including the weekends, for my first three years in the United States. To live comfortably later, some people may need to work more than they would care to today—especially as they acclimate to their new country. Having said that, it's always good to know your goals. Strive to create a life where you don't have to work more than eight hours daily to meet all your financial needs.

Once you master the maximum eight-hour work day, you can focus on even reducing those eight hours and create passive income where you don't have to work to pay your bills. Keep your ears open. You never know who you'll meet or what opportunities might present themselves.

A great time management tip is David Allen's Two Minute Rule: If a task can be done in two minutes or less, you should do it right away.

Postponing tasks of any kind comes with the risk of missing deadlines and forgetting responsibilities. Allowing your to-do list to grow too much also tends to be stressful and overwhelming. Instead, make frequent small efforts and stay on top of things. For example, send out the invite immediately if you just got out of the call and scheduled a one-on-one.

This rule can also be extended toward motivating yourself to accomplish goals. For example, if you take the time to strap on running shoes, you will probably run. Read the first page of a book, and find that the second will follow. The rule can extend to writing, eating healthy foods, or even taking the initiative to speak to a stranger that you find attractive.

Congratulations on finishing Chapter 8!

Use the following questions to help you reflect on the chapter you just read.

1. What mindset has helped you overcome challenges and adapt to life in the USA as an immigrant?

2. List key habits and time management techniques vital for your success in pursuing your ambitions in the USA.

3. How has personal growth influenced your approach to challenges and pursuing the American Dream?

Your progress so far   62%

8/13

CHAPTER 9

PERSONAL FINANCE

As Claire Boothe Luce said, "Money can't buy happiness, but it can make you awfully comfortable while you're being miserable."

This chapter will focus on money-related things, including preservation, accumulation, and inheritance. I honestly wish this knowledge would be taught in schools. It took me almost two decades to learn this information, including its importance.

Many of us come from countries where the banking system is not as advanced as it is in the United States. With the abundance of available credit and things we can buy now and pay for later, immigrants often get overly excited and put themselves in traps where they end up working for the enrichment of credit card companies and financial institutions for years and years.

Understanding the difference between credit and debit is very essential. Here, we will be looking into this and other financial knowledge that will benefit you in your journey to achieving financial freedom.

Most of us have worked or currently work in the service/hospitality industry. I still remember the feeling of gratitude when I would receive a fair amount of tips from a customer or a sense of slight disappointment if the opposite were to happen. I even recall saying then that I would always tip my wait staff fairly when I have money.

This kind of behavior can be noticed by many. A guy who has been a cab driver will likely tip a cab driver a fair amount, and a gal who has waited tables will be inclined to tip her waitress well.

I see this happening all the time. We are often very concerned about tipping our service staff, even pulling out our calculators to ensure we are not shorting the percentage. Yet, for some reason, when it comes to paying a fair amount to those professionals (lawyers, bankers, accountants, insurance agents, etc.) who protect us as we grow, we seem to start penny-pinching and trying to save.

If you think about it, those professionals work hard to keep us out of trouble while presenting us with new opportunities to make and multiply our wealth and assets.

The moral here is to be mindful of your compensation for all who look out for your well-being. Don't get fixed on one industry only, even if it reflects your past.

CASH VS CREDIT

Cash: Simply put, cash money is what you have in your pocket/bank account. In American banking, your money is safely held by your financial institution, available to you whenever you need it, meaning there is no longer any need to keep your cash under the pillow.

American banking and payment systems also eliminate the need to carry large sums of cash on you, leaving you less vulnerable to thieves. Because most transactions are handled online or through debit/credit cards, many Americans don't carry much if any paper money anymore.

In general, it's good to have a small amount of cash with you. You could find yourself in a venue or walking into a smaller local boutique shop where they are not set up to accept credit card payments. I haven't seen many merchants willing to accept personal checks either. Also, it seems like the service staff prefers receiving tips in cash.

Credit: Credit is money you borrow from a financial institution that MUST be repaid, usually with monthly (growing) interest on the remaining unpaid balance. Credit debt can accumulate quickly and becomes increasingly harder to pay back as interest builds.

You may be surprised that banks are usually eager to provide you with a line of credit. I was pleasantly surprised when I first discovered the customer service inherent in the banking industry.

Credit balances usually feature a minimum sum you are expected to pay monthly. While paying the minimum sum will help keep your situation from worsening, it will also lengthen the process. Instead, pay more than the credit card statement recommends as a minimum wherever possible. In doing so, you will clear your debt faster.

However, to borrow in America, it is essential to understand the concept of a "credit score." Your credit score is basically a ranking number that allows lenders to determine how responsible you are with money.

A high credit score will give you access to bigger loans with lower interest rates. A low credit score, on the other hand, will limit your borrowing potential while forcing you to accept higher interest rates.

With that in mind and considering the importance of credit in modern society, even a bad credit score is better than no credit score at all. Apply for a credit card right away to begin building your score. You may find that, initially, it is hard to find an institution willing to provide you with a credit card.

If that is your situation, consider getting a "secured card"--a credit card backed up with your own cash. In other words, if you put down $500, the card company will provide a line of credit equal to that sum.

As you pay the balance off, you will build a credit score, allowing you to eventually borrow more significant sums of money.

The most important rule with credit cards is to never spend more than you can pay back at the end of the month (billing cycle). Not only does this preserve your credit score, but it also helps you avoid interest.

While this effectively makes your credit card no different than a debit card, there are reasons to have both. Besides the fact that credit cards help you build a credit score, they also give you access to large sums of money in case of an emergency. For example, say a major appliance breaks suddenly, or there is an emergency hospitalization. In these situations, credit cards are a valuable source of ready cash.

As we discussed in the Best Mindset section, you are getting yourself ready for when winter comes. Having access to money when you need it is a very comforting feeling. Not to mention the rewards and incentives ("ethical bribes") that credit card companies will start offering you as your credit improves. If you think about it, you get money back in the form of rewards for using someone else's money temporarily for the purchases you need so long as you are disciplined enough to pay the outstanding balance at the end of the billing cycle.

For example, after seven years of using a Chase Visa credit card with rewards, I accumulated enough points for two people to travel for free! It's like someone else is buying and granting me an all-inclusive vacation for using their money temporarily for my daily purchases!

Other card companies provide similar rewards. By carefully selecting your credit card and paying on it responsibly, you can enjoy a similar experience. I am not promoting Chase credit cards here. The example illustrates the power of correctly using a rewards credit card. Do your research before you select a card. They all come with their set of pros and cons.

A strange observation is that your chances of being approved for the card you want increase drastically if you wait for them to send you a pre-approval offer (which usually comes in the mail) and then apply.

CREDIT SCORES

Credit scores are, arguably, as essential as your personal history. I recommend you carefully watch after the health and well-being of your credit score. This means paying your bills on time, not maxing out (spending to the limit) your credit cards unnecessarily, and reviewing your credit report once in a while for fraudulent charges and suggestions to improve.

A good credit score means quicker and cheaper access to capital when and if needed. And this alone will provide peace of mind knowing you have access to funds in case of emergency or business/venture expansion.

A credit score of 700 and above is usually considered good.[10] The higher your score goes, the better it's.

There are three major agencies that rank people's credit and they are Equifax *(www.equifax.com)*, Experian *(www.experian.com)*, and Transunion *(www.transunion.com)*. Credit scores can range anywhere between 300 and 850.

How do they determine your score?

1. Past payment history - How well have you paid off outstanding balances in the past?

2. Amounts owed - How much debt do you currently have?

3. Length of time - How long have you been using your credit?

4. Newly opened and outstanding credits - How many accounts do you have open?

5. Credit mix - What types of accounts do you have: credit cards, mortgages, auto loans, HELOCs, etc.?

---

[10]   "What Is a Good Credit Score? - NerdWallet." https://www.nerd-wallet.com/article/finance/what-is-a-good-credit-score. Accessed 16 Apr. 2022.

I can proudly say that I have been responsible for my credit lines since the start. I have always paid them off in time and never tried to max out my credit. On numerous occasions, I have leveraged my good credit score during negotiations with financial institutions and individuals for larger purchases, business deals, and/or access to higher credit lines.

Contrary to that, my former roommate, Javier, had trouble obtaining credit after filing for bankruptcy. The process was discouraging, and the interest rates offered were astronomical.

Bankruptcies will stay on your credit report for seven years or more. Whenever possible, avoid filing for bankruptcy. In life, emergencies happen, and if you must carry a balance forward for the next few months until you can get back on your feet, that's okay. That's what the credit lines are for. However, you must always pay the indicated minimum balance monthly. Credit card companies will start reporting to credit bureaus if you fail to keep up with your minimum balance payments.

The most common reason people's credit score is low and obtaining credit on good terms is difficult is late or missed payments.

Credit card companies will remain at bay if you keep meeting your minimum monthly payments as they make money from you each month you carry a balance. These credit card companies love customers who allow interest to build up. The best way is to pay the minimum required balance plus a little more toward the principal balance. This way, you are lowering your outstanding balance each month, including the amount of interest you end up paying.

Try thinking about the credit offered as borrowed money from a friend, not a large corporation. That way of thinking helps me not overspend the funds available and keep paying the balance off each month diligently, as I don't want to let my "friend" down for borrowing the money when I need it. If you think about it, it's an actual win-win-win-win scenario:

1. You are not accumulating debt.

2. You are building up your credit score.

3. You are not risking your own money if your credit card is lost, stolen, or hacked.

4. You are accumulating perks assuming your card is a rewards card. On top of points and cashback, some offer additional benefits such as an extended warranty for purchased products, insurance for additional drivers for rented vehicles, ticket cancellation policies, etc.

Many credit card companies have systems in place to proactively watch for fraud and will alert the customer before they even know something's wrong. If you lose your card or suspect it was stolen or hacked, report it immediately to the financial institution by calling them. Write down the agent's name you speak to and brief notes from the conversation. If your credit card has been used without your authorization don't panic, credit card companies will investigate the charge and reimburse any unauthorized charges.

Get into the habit of paying with credit cards when possible. There were instances when a merchant I have dealt with didn't deliver the service and/or goods yet charged my card or overcharged. All I had to do was to submit a claim with my credit card company to get reimbursed.

Keep building up your credit score, and in time you will find yourself benefiting from it in ways you can't even foresee right now.

By law, you can obtain a free credit report once a year by visiting *www.annualcreditreport.com*.

STOCKS

In general, stocks beat the market. On average, you get 8%-10% on your money over long periods of time. The key is to have your money in the market for an extended time. I am talking decades, not months or even years. Don't invest in the stock market if you think you will need or may need money in the near future. If you sell your stocks when they are low, you are losing out on the actual stock price (the difference between what you paid when you bought minus what you sold it for) and the potential gains the stocks will make down the road. No one can time the market, and trying to beat an individual stock is similar to gambling.

The key is discipline and balance. Your portfolio should be well-balanced and diversified. Some financial institutions do this better than others.

In general, these are three main ways to invest:

1. Hedge funds - Managed portfolios tailored, in general, for the ultra-wealthy.
2. Mutual funds - Created for working-class people such as you and I. Like hedge funds, they are actively

managed. The problem here comes in the form of fees from buying and trading. Financial institutions push these funds because they are quite profitable to them.

3. Index funds - Fixed accounts, traded only a handful of times. They have small fees, thus, in general, they deliver the best ROI (return on investment) over the long term.

You can invest in individual corporations or have a diversified portfolio with stocks. Overall, a diversified portfolio is a safer route unless you are very familiar with the stock market or plan to learn "day trading."

I started investing in stocks before investing in cryptocurrency because stocks are less volatile. This helped me build up my immunity to sudden market moves. However, especially at the beginning, there were times when I thought it would be easier to sell what little I had left and exit the market altogether, so I stopped experiencing the overwhelming pain. Due to the correct advice, research, and intuition, I stuck through the hard times, and, as was expected, the stocks moved back into the green with refreshed power, creating even more capital gains. Unfortunately, some of my even close-circle friends couldn't handle the volatility and ended up selling their stocks and taking heavy losses.

Generally, my index portfolio with Charles Schwab *(www.schwab.com)* has been performing better than the individual stocks I picked, except for a few outliers. If you are like me and don't have time, energy, or desire to learn and monitor the market closely, the best strategy would be to invest in an index fund and keep depositing a fixed monthly amount. Let your money grow over time.

If you consider yourself a person with higher risk-reward tolerance, try this strategy: pick a person whose life mission resonates with you and start buying their company's stocks monthly. The purchase amount can be a fixed dollar amount or number of shares, regardless of the share price. You will have stocks accumulated in time, and due to ingenuity, problem-solving, and mass adoption, those stock prices should go up. This is a double win for you, assuming you picked the right candidate to invest in. For example, I like Elon Musk's work and invest in Tesla stocks. Another person may say the same about Steve Jobs and Apple stocks. Imagine how wealthy you would be right now if you had bought Apple or Tesla stocks when they just launched.

Test various strategies for a year or two. Find which works best for you, and then double down on it.

SO WHAT IS DAY TRADING?

Day trading is the practice of buying and selling given assets on the same day to gain profits from short-term price variations. Day traders usually sell out all of their securities on the same day to avoid the risk of market fluctuations overnight.

Given the increasing options of online trading software, day trading has become more accessible.

For most of us, day trading is not a viable option as we already have our professions and financial responsibilities for our loved ones. As with any other skill, day trading takes time to learn and carries high expenses and high risk.

It's never too late to start investing. Of course, the earlier you start, the better the ROI. This example from Ramsey Solutions[11] provides a great potential earnings scenario:

Compound interest is a millionaire's best friend. It's free money. Seriously. But don't take our word for it—let us introduce you to our friends Steven and John.

When Steven turned 21, he decided to start investing $200 a month every year for nine years. At age 30, he decided to stop investing altogether. But his friend John started when Steven stopped, investing $200 a month every month starting at age 30, all the way until the ripe old age of 68.

So at age 68, who do you think had more money in their account? Let's do the math.

At the end of nine years, Steven invested $21,600, didn't invest another dime, and ended up with close to $2.35 million at age 68. Let's say that again—$2.35 million! That's the power of compound interest, friends.

And Steven's friend John invested a whopping $91,200 over the course of 37 years. At age 68, he had built up $1.3 million, but he never caught up with Steven.

So how did Steven do it? He didn't invest nearly as much as John did but ended up with over $1 million more. That's the power of compound interest! It turns more than $20,000 invested in nine short years into almost $2.35 million over 37 years!

---

[11] "How Teens Can Become Millionaires | RamseySolutions.com." 14 Dec. 2021, https://www.ramseysolutions.com/retirement/how-teens-can-become-millionaires. Accessed 4 Mar. 2022.

Consider consulting with a financial advisor. Also, be aware that not every so-called financial advisor is on your side.

The following book is written with easy to understand language and will help you get your feet wet: *Unshakeable: Your Financial Freedom Playbook* by Tony Robbins with Peter Mallouk.

CRYPTOCURRENCY

Before diving into cryptocurrency (crypto), let's briefly refresh our memories about the history of money. This exercise can help us analyze where the money was and where it could go.

What is money? As we all know, money is a medium of exchange.

In the beginning, humans used a barter system, which is essentially exchanging services and goods for other services and goods. The system outdated itself, as one only needs so many chairs, right?

Then came commodity money, the currency in physical forms, such as gold, silver, crops, etc. Those items were scarce, and thus were accepted universally.

Representative money—tablets, coins—followed. Since they were quite cumbersome to transport, especially in large quantities, promissory notes were created, which became the first form of paper money. Once the paper promissory notes reached Europe, banks started issuing them in the form of banknotes.

People started to move from paper money to accounting currency, credit cards, bank transfers, etc. The government and financial institutions maintain control at all times, effectively keeping money centralized.

The idea behind crypto is to decentralize currency so it cannot be overissued, and everyone has the right to keep accounts. This is why Bitcoin (BTC), the very first crypto, was created by Satoshi Nakamoto. It's not attached to any government and doesn't have a central issuing authority or a regulatory body. It decentralizes the entire system, takes control and accountability from the government, and gives it to the people. Crypto is an entirely new medium of exchange: digital currency.

BTC is a currency backed by nothing, as mentioned above, there is no government, commodity, or company standing behind it. BTC's price is driven by supply, demand, and speculation. The more folks want it, the more expensive it becomes. It's also limited in quantity and thus scarce. If everyone decided to opt out of accepting BTC as a form of payment, BTC's value would instantly vanish.

After BTC, alternative coins (altcoins) were developed: e.g., Ethereum (Ether), ADA Cardano, Solana, and the list goes on.

These altcoins were created using a decentralized platform, on which decentralized apps (dApps) can be created to solve an existing problem. The alternative platforms accept their own native currency as a form of payment to use the platform or exchange goods and services. That is, the Ether platform accepts Ether currency as payment. Unlike BTC, most altcoins aim to solve some existing problems, such as inefficient payment networks, academic performance tracking, etc. Some altcoins are partnering with governments to streamline payment networks and improve student academic tracking.

Non-fungible tokens (NFTs), which on a basic level are a verification of a digital or physical item such as real estate, music, art, etc., are even being considered as modern-day collectibles. They are traded online, with asset ownership verified and recorded in a digital ledger in a blockchain, which is the exact technology behind cryptocurrencies. Imagine how much time and money can be saved if one can instantly purchase a house, or even a portion of a house, without a lengthy title and legal work process?

It is noteworthy to mention that El Salvador is the first country to adopt Bitcoin as its currency. As of September 2021, Salvadorans can pay their taxes and purchase goods and services with bitcoin.

Cryptocurrency is a new technology, and some suggest it will eventually replace the banking system as we know it, especially with the development of decentralized finance (DeFi), which removes the control financial institutions and banks have over money.

Looking back in history, we see that money has constantly been evolving. New and improved eventually take over old and outdated. I believe decentralized crypto has a shot at taking over the centralized, traditional banking system.

As more countries follow the El Salvadorian example, cryptocurrency may eventually prove to be a very worthwhile investment.

Should you decide to invest in crypto, make sure you know exactly what you are doing. Launched in 2009, BTC is the oldest and largest by market share of digital currency.

BTC is referred to as digital gold and is the most recognized name. Bitcoin is also a market mover. The altcoins go up shortly after BTC starts going up, and they follow the same pattern when BTC is losing its strength. Interestingly enough, since altcoins are less stable, they seem to deliver higher-percentage gains when BTC is up and, subsequently, greater losses when BTC is down.

Like with any other investment, the timing of when to buy or sell and the patience to hold the asset despite market panic are determining factors in crypto investing. I have heard of people who became millionaires and billionaires just by investing in crypto. I have also heard of some folks who lost all of their savings because they got into it at the wrong time and, more importantly, with the wrong mindset.

The more educated and informed you are about the crypto world, the higher your chances of getting impressive returns on your investment. Watch the world climate. Stocks and crypto markets react poorly to uncertainty. It may be worth waiting out if you see another pandemic, interstate conflict, global supply chain problem, or other drastic event unfolding.

I personally invest in cryptocurrency, and when markets are down 60% or more, I may refuse to look at my account's cash value, so I am not tempted to sell. Innovation and adoption are happening rapidly in the sector, which means it should turn out to be a solid investment in due time. Crypto investing may not be for you if you haven't built up an immunity to market volatility.

Rule of thumb, don't invest more than you can stomach. The key is not to panic sell, especially when markets are tanking. Make sure you won't need the funds you invest in the foreseeable future. You will lose twofold if you have to sell your assets because you need cash when the markets are down: one, because you are selling it for less than what you had paid for it, and, two, you miss out on any potential future gains. Suppose the project you invested in truly solves an existing problem, serves as a utility for many, and has a mass following. In that case, it will likely come back around and prove to be a profitable investment.

Utilize as many tools as possible to leverage your positions, such as the Crypto Fear & Greed Index, Relative Strength Index (RSI), Bitcoin Exchange Balance, Bitcoin Dominance Index Chart.

I want to reiterate that thorough research and patience are key. The better your entry point, the quicker you see returns on your investments. Since no one can time the market, dollar-cost-averaging (DCA), steadily buying a certain amount of crypto (or stocks) for a specific time period, seems to work best.

Never feel pressured and do not act because of fear of losing out (FOMO). If you are patient and strategic, you will come across another buying or selling opportunity in time.

BUYING VS RENTING

Upon arrival in Maryland, I started renting a room at my cousin's house. It was cheaper and logistically easier while the rent was helping out my cousin with his mortgage payments. Everyone benefited.

Once I built up enough momentum, I moved out and started renting a one-bedroom apartment. By then, I had been steadily working at three jobs and had paid off the private car loan I had borrowed from a friend.

After a while, I relocated into a three-bedroom, three-bathroom townhouse in Baltimore for $1,200 per month. I then sublet each bedroom at $400 per month, which would bring in $800 per month in rent. So, technically, for only $400 a month, I would have "the entire" townhouse, plus the basement where I set up my office and started my first business.

Many newcomers will likely go through the same steps, contingent upon their circumstances, such as family size, available funds, and living standards.

Nowadays, searching online is the best place to find apartments for rent. Websites such as Zillow (*www.zillow.com*), Apartments (*www.apartments.com*), ApartmentGuide (*www.apartmentguide.com*), ApartmentFinder (*www.apartmentfinder.com*), and Rent (*www.rent.com*) seem to be popular.

Here is the essential list of documents required, although it is worth noting that a leasing office will have its own guidelines and may require additional paperwork:

- Income verification, usually, most recent pay stubs.
- Employment verification, which is typically a signed statement on company letterhead.
- Photo identification (e.g., driver's license, passport, green card).
- Social security number.
- Bank statements.

Putting aside demand, whether you will be allowed to rent the apartment and the amount of the down payment will be determined by your credit reports and rental history. The leasing office will pull those reports.

If your credit score is not yet qualified, they may require a cosigner and/or a higher deposit amount.

When living in an apartment complex, be mindful of the noise level, especially after regular working hours. Some complexes might forbid smoking anywhere on the premises too. In Uzbekistan, loud sounds and noise are created to notify the neighbors about the newlyweds after the wedding. This happens right before the bride enters her new house. Following the tradition, we attempted to do it in America. Well, as you may imagine, it didn't work out well with the neighbors and authorities.

While shopping for your next home, be sure to ask your leasing or property manager about parking and common area usage rules, such as laundry, playground, pool, pet areas, etc.

In general, tenants are responsible for paying utilities and the internet. Landlords usually pay for trash pick up, landscaping, roof leaks, HVAC, and water. There is usually a 24-hour minimum entry notice requirement unless there is an emergency like a flood, fire, etc. Get yourself familiarized with the terms and conditions of your rental agreement.

One-year rent is generally cheaper than semiannual and month-to-month rent.

You cannot be rejected to rent or purchase based on your race, religion, color, sex, family status, disability, or national origin. Under the Fair Housing Act, everyone is equally protected against housing discrimination.[12]

If you ever experience housing discrimination, you can file a complaint following this link: *www.hud.gov/ program_offices/fair_housing_equal_opp/online-complaint.*

While renting is very common in the United States, my perspective has always been that it's similar to burning your money. Why? Because when you vacate your lease, you're left with no tangible assets.

Here is an example from my experience: I rented a house for $1,250 monthly in Baltimore. I moved five years later when I was able to purchase my first house. In those five years, I had paid $75,000 to my landlord! All this money spent provided me with a shelter, but it didn't allow me to build any equity.

Unfortunately, renting is usually unavoidable as you save to buy a house. Most of the time, you want to be able to put down 20% of the purchasing price when you select a home. In doing so, you can avoid private mortgage insurance (PMI), which protects the lender only but not yourself if you cannot pay your mortgage.

That said, if you want to begin building equity as quickly as possible, you may still buy a home by putting down 3%-5%. Once you have paid off 20% of the mortgage, you will then be able to drop the PMI.

I purchased my first house by putting down 3% (30-year mortgage) because I needed my cash to improve the house.

---

[12]   "Housing Discrimination Under the Fair Housing Act - HUD." https://www.hud.gov/program_offices/fair_housing_equal_opp/ fair_housing_act_overview. Accessed 17 Apr. 2022.

I then took advantage of Fannie Mae and Freddie Mac's 3% down payment program.

Since both are government-owned programs, they require a homeowner to have PMI insurance. After the improvements, my house value went up. Then I refinanced and took out a 15-year mortgage; my payment went up less than $50 a month because I could drop the PMI and save hundreds of dollars monthly. I converted the loan into a conventional loan (no longer government guaranteed). Since my value went up, I was able to reach the threshold of 20% percent and thus could opt out of PMI insurance payments.

This worked out very well for me, but keep in mind that every situation is different.

Just by paying $100 more toward the principal balance on a $200,000, 30-year fixed mortgage you will save yourself 4.5 years,[13] not to mention a ton of money on interest payments that otherwise would have gone to your lender.

Another benefit of purchasing a home is that you always have the option to rent or sell it. You will not need to pay the home off before you can move.

MAKING MONEY VS BUILDING WEALTH

There is a difference between making money and building wealth. Of course, you should first learn how to make money as it's literally impossible to build wealth without some start-up capital or the means to acquire it.

---

[13] "Loan amortization and extra mortgage payments - Wells Fargo." https://www.wellsfargo.com/financial-education/homeownership/ loan-amortization-extra-payments/. Accessed 4 Mar. 2022.

Here is an example that illustrates the difference between making money and building wealth:

- Buy and Flip - You buy a house, rehab it, and sell it. For simplicity, let's say you buy the house for $100,000, your rehab/renovation costs are $50,000, and you sell the house for $200,000. You just made $50,000 profit (minus the closing costs, agent fees, taxes, recording fees, etc., of course).

- Buy and Hold - You buy a house for $100,000, put in $50,000 to increase its value. Now your house is worth $200,000 ([ARV] after repair value). You refinance your house at 75% LTV (loan to value), exactly $150,000 (plus the closing cost, taxes, agent fees, recording fees, etc., of course).

  Your mortgage at 5%, 15-year fixed for a $150,000 loan is roughly $1,186 + $250 for taxes and insurance.

  You rent the house for $1,800 per month.

  $1,186 + $250 (taxes and insurance) = $1,436 (net monthly operating cost).

  $1,800 (rent) - $1,436 (operating cost) = $364 (profit) per month (passive income).

  Indeed, in this scenario, we are simplifying transactions for illustration purposes.

  Of course, $364 per month income compared to $50,000 from the first scenario may seem like a joke. Yet here are the not-so-obvious advantages of the Buy and Hold strategy:

- Someone else is paying off your debt!
- You are making a passive income of $4,368 per year.
- In fifteen years, the house will be yours free and clear. Most likely it will go up in value as well. Your $200,000 house may eventually be worth $250,000 if not more.
- The house then becomes an asset you can leave to your children, or liquidate when the time comes.

Once the house is paid off, the rent becomes money in your pocket. Let's say it didn't increase (which is highly unlikely), and you are still collecting $1,800 per month.

$1,800 - $250 (taxes and insurance) = $1,550 rental income as you don't have to pay the mortgage to your bank anymore. That's $1,550 x 12 = $18,600 income per year!

And of course, the more you invest in rental properties, the more your wealth will expand over time.

For example, if you were able to accumulate ten rental properties in your lifetime free and clear, then do the math! Your net worth just skyrocketed to $2,000,000 + and your passive income to $186,000 per year without the need to work full time! The other option is for you to hire a property management company but that will cut into your profits.

As you can see, in the Buy and Flip scenario, the money was made quickly and in a large sum, but it was only made once. However, it can also be spent just as quickly.

One may argue that theoretically, you can buy and flip over and over and keep making a profit of $50K a pop. And if you can manage multiple flips at a time, you can clear even more.

And there are some well-oiled machines out there that flip houses left and right and make a ton of money. However, flipping a property is not the kind of thing most will likely do very often because it requires a series of moving parts to work seamlessly, including market conditions that no one can control.

I can say that enormous pressure from flipping multiple properties simultaneously tested my partnership and friendship with Jose. At times, Jose ended up literally swinging the hammer daily with the crew, and I would cover the office and Home Depot runs. Ultimately, this endeavor took up too much time, money, and energy. Luckily, with determination and countless hours of work while keeping our heads cool, we safely navigated the waters, although the toll it took was apparent.

Compare this to buying and renting, which we have going for us as a true part-time investment. The key here is to learn how to create multiple passive income streamlines. It's not about making a lot of money in one shot, it's more about having a little bit of money coming in from different streams, continuously, while letting your assets grow in value. This is what I call a wise investment.

Other examples of passive income sources include diversified stocks, businesses that run without your active involvement, art pieces that go up in value, and patents.

HEALTH INSURANCE

Health insurance is of enormous importance. We are sometimes so obsessed with having our "new toys" insured. We buy additional insurance to protect them in case of an emergency.

Yet if you think about it, none of those things would exist without you because you are the one who earned the money to purchase them. Therefore, I believe it's important to insure yourself before insuring your latest cellphone or laptop.

It's like insuring golden eggs for accidental damage while forgetting to insure the hen that lays those golden eggs. Without the hen, there would be no golden eggs at all.

The cost of health insurance in the United States is indeed very high. It is also true that the system is flawed and heavily criticized. Ultimately, however, having insurance allows you to live a healthier life, secure in the fact that you will be taken care of in the event of a medical emergency.

One may purchase health insurance through an employer or as an individual. Ask about plans offered and contribution levels if your employer offers health insurance. You can purchase it individually if you are not employed or your employer doesn't offer a health plan.

Even if your employer offers health insurance, it doesn't hurt to check out other plans offered at HealthCare.Gov (*www.healthcare.gov*), as in some instances, the plans offered at HealthCare.Gov are either cheaper or offer better coverage.

If you need help navigating through the paperwork, there is most likely an agent within your community who speaks your language.

You may even qualify for federal or state health assistance programs based on your income and circumstances.

Use this link to see available plans in your area: *www.finder.healthcare.gov.*

If you need help locating a local insurance broker or agent, check this out: *www.healthcare.gov/find-assistance.*

You may also consider putting money into a health savings account (HSA), which can be invested in stocks in the event that you do not use all of your medical allotments. If you are relatively healthy, feel free to invest the yearly max allowed (tax-free) into your HSA. Then simply move that money into a participating investment account. In this instance, you are not only insured but also seeing your funds grow in a tax-free space.

If you have a health emergency, dial 911. This is the fastest way to request medical help. One time, when I was having excruciating pain related to kidney stones, they sent firefighters to pick me up. Firefighters usually have paramedics and adequately trained personnel to perform emergency medical services.

In some extreme situations, when every minute is to be counted, 911 may even dispatch helicopters to get the patient to the hospital.

The great thing about U.S. medicine and its doctors is that they will do everything to save a life. The flip side of the coin is all this will cost money and eventually be billed to the patient and the patient's insurance.

The more personnel and transportation involved during the emergency, the higher the bill. The bill will go to collections if unpaid, negatively affecting your credit score.

If your situation is not dire, and you have someone to take you to a hospital, I suggest you take that route and go into an emergency room or urgent care.

Also, be aware that although emergency rooms are called emergency rooms, they are usually packed to capacity. Based on your particular case, you may find yourself waiting for hours and hours just to be seen by a doctor because they always prioritize those in worse situations.

I find local urgent care centers such as Patient First, Right Time, and Kaiser Permanente to be quicker and cost less.

Most communities have at least one healthcare facility, aka clinics or community health centers, which provide free or low-cost services.

The Department of Health and Human Services funds many of those facilities to provide basic health care to immigrants. To find a doctor near you, go to the following website: *www.findahealthcenter.hrsa.gov*.

Staying proactive with your health, that is, regular check-ups with your doctor, eating healthy, sleeping well, and regularly exercising, is the best approach. I realize things happen in our lives, and at times we deemphasize our health. I strongly urge you not to neglect your health and listen to your body as closely as possible. Something that seems small can turn into something urgent and costly. I even know of a situation when a toothache ignored for years turned into cancer and cost a loved one's life, which devastated the entire family.

They advise putting the oxygen mask on yourself first during an airplane emergency and then helping others. You're limited with how much you can help others if sick, starving, or poor. That is why your personal health and well-being come first!

PLANNED PARENTHOOD

Planned Parenthood is a nonprofit that offers sexual health-care education and affordable health services. Its services include, yet are not limited to, preventative care such as birth control, sexually transmitted infection testing and treatment, abortion, screening for cervical and other cancers, etc. To learn more and get qualified help, visit their website via the following link: *www.plannedparenthood.org*.

LIFE INSURANCE

Like making a will, life insurance is morbid, uncomfortable, and very important. If you are the sole breadwinner in your home, having life insurance means that your loved ones will be taken care of in the event of your death.

There are two main types of life insurance policies: temporary and permanent.

As the name goes, temporary life insurance covers for a limited period, such as 10, 20, or 30 years. Assuming the tragic event didn't occur, the insurance company profits from all those payments as there is nothing to pay out for. Truthfully, this is a much better outcome for the insured as well.

Permanent life insurance policies are usually more expensive, but they have the benefit of contributing to funeral expenses. They can also be tapped for assisted living costs, borrowing money against the account's cash value, or even retirement, as some generate interest over time.

Like health insurance, life insurance can be purchased via an employer or agent/broker, and unlike health insurance, there is no single resource, which means you will have to do your own research.

When selecting your life insurance company, make sure to go with the reputable one. The last thing you want is for the company to go out of business before you actually need those funds.

In general, it is advised that you have a policy that will cover at least 5x your annual earnings.

The rule of thumb, the earlier you get your life insurance set up, the lower monthly rates you will get locked into.

Just to put some numbers into perspective[14]:

A temporary $500,000 life insurance policy for a 30-year-old man is $18.91 per month, whereas for a 50-year-old male is $69.58 monthly.

---

[14] "Life Insurance Buying Guide: Types, Companies and Quotes." https://www.nerdwallet.com/a/insurance/life-insurance. Accessed 17 Apr. 2022.

The same coverage amount for permanent life insurance for a 30-year-old man is $359 per month compared to $822.91 for a 50-year-old man.

I bought a life insurance policy when my first daughter was born. None of us would like to plan or talk about the day we die. Yet we all realize that death comes for all of us. Trust me, you will feel much better once the policy is in place, knowing that in case of a tragic event, your loved ones are taken care of, at least financially.

As mentioned, permanent life insurance offers interest accounts. If you are able to opt into one, then perhaps looking at it as another investment vehicle may help.

My parents tried to push me to cancel my insurance policy after I had told them about it. In their eyes, by preparing a will in advance, I would jinx myself and could possibly expedite my death.

Their reaction is understandable, considering their background and the superstitions they were steeped in. They found peace after I invited them to look at it as a savings plan because I don't have to die to use it, and I can actually withdraw the funds at a specific age, and it accumulates a percentage like the stocks all that time.

Deep inside, I felt at peace knowing that my loved ones are protected in case of a tragedy. This feeling, I must admit, is comforting.

529 COLLEGE SAVINGS PLANS

One of my business partners, Jose Henriquez, calls education the modern form of slavery. Colleges are commercialized, overpriced, and in need of government regulation.

In the past, enslaved people didn't have the luxury of changing their masters or taking vacations or enjoying any other benefits we take for granted nowadays. However, those who graduate from modern colleges with debt are forced to work to pay off their student loans. And in some cases, they must pay for decades because sometimes those sums have drifted well into the six figures

Sadly, the interest rates for college debt are incredibly high, double digits compared to other forms of loans, such as mortgages or auto loans.

Unlike mortgages, student debt cannot be refinanced, which means you can't go to a different lender, i.e., "master," and can't even be written off even in case of bankruptcy. In short, there is no escape from college debt. It will always be in your history, always accumulating interest as time passes.

From an entrepreneurial perspective, it's like robbing you of your better future, as you may not be able to start your own business just because you can't take a break from making those monthly student loan payments.

Only 27% of graduates end up working in the field that they earned a degree in, and an even smaller percentage of them are happy at what they do.[15]

As an employer, I can tell you that I pay more attention to candidates' experiences and attitudes than their education. Most of my entrepreneur friends hold a similar attitude.

---

[15] "Only 27 percent of college grads have a job related to their major." 20 May 2013, https://www.washingtonpost.com/news/wonk/wp/2013/05/20/only-27-percent-of-college-grads-have-a-job-related-to-their-major/. Accessed 19 Nov. 2021.

None of this is to discourage you from getting an education. In general, the educated population tends to do the most to change the world and usually finds higher-paying jobs. It's all about how you approach higher education.

If you are a parent, consider investing in a 529 college savings plan early on for your child(ren). Create a discipline of monthly installments. The other advantage is that the federal government allows up to a certain amount of tax-free contributions per child per year, assuming those funds are used in the future for the child's education.

At the time of this writing, the 529 deduction limit is $2,500 per child per year.

I see education as a much more valuable gift to the next generation than simply leaving them an inheritance. Money can be wasted and lost. On the other hand, education allows children the chance to carve out their own niche and thrive in it. This particular statement may sound contradictory to what I am saying above, so let me elaborate a little more.

Some fields, such as medicine and law, require intensive secondary education before one can even attain entry. Other industries, such as software, transportation, or hospitality, don't necessarily require a four-year college degree and beyond to enter.

Since we can only guide our kids toward a specific profession, we can't be sure which one they will end up pursuing when the time comes.

I would rather start saving for my child's future college plan now, even if they eventually decide not to attend college. The good news is that those funds can be used to pay for online courses and certifications with eligible institutions. This means, regardless of the field your children choose to go into, you know, as a parent, that you have saved up enough funds to give them a solid headstart with limited to no debt.

Note that a 529 plan is an investment plan with tax advantages to encourage savings for future education. If you are a student trying to get assistance from the government for your education, refer to Chapter 6: "The Power of Language" for the steps to apply for student aid.

As parents, our goals should be twofold when it comes to our children's education: (1) allow our children the chance to find the educational opportunity that is right for them and (2) help make sure that they aren't buried under mountains of debt in the process.

PREPARING FOR RETIREMENT

Unfortunately, U.S. retirement policy is not the best.[16] Therefore, it's your responsibility to prepare yourself and guarantee your own retirement.

It's never too early or too late to start getting ready for your retirement! Needless to say, the sooner you start, the more comfortably you will retire. Remember our friend Steven who started putting money away at age 21?

Keeping money in your pillow, or even in a regular savings account, is like slowly burning a percentage of your money each month. In the end, due to inflation, you

---

[16] "System is 'flawed' when most Americans have tiny retirement savings." 12 Dec. 2019, https://www.cnbc.com/2019/12/12/system-is-flawed-when-most-americans-have-tiny-retirement-savings.html. Accessed 4 Mar. 2022.

actually end up losing money. You should always anticipate things you need to do to stay above inflation. Stocks are time-tested methods for doing that.

401(K) PLAN

A 401(K) is a retirement savings plan with tax advantages many American employers offer. The name comes after a section of the U.S. Internal Revenue Code.

By signing up for a 401(K), you agree to have a percentage of each paycheck directly deposited into an investment account of your choice among several investment options, usually mutual funds.

Take advantage of 401(K)s benefits if your employer offers them. This is a great way to start putting away money for your retirement. The best part is that, often, your employer will match your contribution level!

These contributions are tax-deductible and can be tax-deferred.

If you are self-employed or your employer doesn't offer a 401(K) plan, consider opening an Individual Retirement Account (IRA).

Although, it is worth mentioning that, in many cases, IRA contributions tax deductibility is lesser. The good news is that the contributions can be made up by April 15th of the following year.

RETIREMENT ACCOUNTS

Do you remember the ant and the grasshopper parable? The ant worked all summer in preparation for winter, whereas the grasshopper did not consider its future and only lived for today. Not sure about you, but I would instead follow the ant's strategy.

One of the ways to do it is by contributing funds now so your future self can enjoy and thank you later when the time comes.

Let's first look at the aforementioned IRA.

An IRA is an account that encourages saving for retirement by providing various tax advantages.

There are two major retirement accounts: traditional IRA and Roth IRA. Here are the main differences:

- *Traditional* - your contributions are pre- or after tax. The invested money grows tax-deferred. All withdrawals are taxed as current income after the age of 59 1/2.
- *Roth* - your contributions are after-tax. Your investment grows tax-free. In general, you can withdraw the money tax-free and penalty-free after the age of 59 1/2.

Generally, Roth IRAs are best suited for individuals who expect to be in a higher tax bracket at retirement age. Traditional IRAs are better suited for those who expect to be in the same or lower tax bracket.

PREPARING A WILL

Having a will is not necessarily about getting ready for death. It's more about reducing the potential for chaos in the event that you pass away unexpectedly. The process of making a will may be uncomfortable, but the results are worth it. Having a will makes it clear who should get what after you are gone.

It may also include information on what should happen to you and your assets in the event that you are alive but no longer in a position to make decisions for yourself.

It's also worth mentioning that creating a will doesn't have to be very difficult. With low membership fees, services such as LegalShield (*www.legalshield.com*) usually include drafting a will at no additional cost.

Congratulations on finishing Chapter 9!

Use the following questions to help you reflect on the chapter you just read.

1. When imagining your ideal home, what key features matter most? This includes architectural style (condo, townhouse, single-family), room and bathroom count, outdoor spaces like patio or backyard, and other essentials.

2. Where do you intend to initially live upon arriving in the U.S.? Have you researched housing options that match your preferences?

3. What age do you plan to retire? Have you created a solid retirement plan to ensure financial security and satisfaction in your retirement years?

Your progress so far   69%

9/13

CHAPTER 10

EMPLOYMENT & WORKING FOR YOURSELF

In this chapter, we will primarily examine what to do to start your own business. We will discuss a winning mindset, partnerships to forge, types of common entities to consider, how to negotiate with financial institutions, and more.

However, despite America being a fertile environment for small businesses, not everyone in this country—immigrant or otherwise—dreams of becoming an entrepreneur. Hundreds of other options exist, including working as a manager/executive at somebody else's well-run company.

I know some executives who were able to find the right organization and now earn more money than average entrepreneurs while having more freedom and better control of their time. They have impressive benefits packages and a solid company backing them. If that is you, then more power to you. If you find a great company where you can grow while keeping a healthy work-life balance, feel free to stay with that organization and make it your home.

Toward that, in the first two sections, we will talk about best practices when you work for someone else and how to find employment. Regardless of which route you end up taking, make sure it works best for you and those you love first.

I find that the job search process, including the work ethic, is different in the States compared to Uzbekistan. Granted, who you know makes a difference regardless of what country you are in. However, when you relocate to a new country, your circle of friends and those you know will most likely be limited. The good news in the States is that you don't have to know or bribe someone to get a job. Your qualifications, intentions, and persistence alone can get you far in this country.

WORKING FOR EMPLOYERS

In America, as in many other parts of the world, success in the workplace requires striking a fine balance. Part of this balance requires doing simple things correctly every time you show up for work.

Full-time jobs are commonly understood as five days and forty hours per week in eight-hour shifts, usually Monday through Friday. Generally, anything above thirty-two hours a week is considered a full-time position, although laws differ state by state. Full-time positions typically come with benefits such as health insurance, 401K retirement plan, life insurance, vacation pay, holiday pay, and sick leave.

The benefits and contribution packages are determined by an employer and will be referenced in the employee handbook. Make sure to go through the handbook in detail, as it will also outline other important policies such as code of conduct, dress code, reporting, grievances, etc. Do take advantage of the offered benefits and comply with the rest of the company policies.

Depending upon your industry of choice, you may be asked to work weekends, holidays, nights, and evenings. I worked graveyard shifts, holidays, and weekends while cleaning a store, even after switching to the hospitality industry. I was young, unmarried, and without kids. Therefore, I was okay with putting in those hours.

During the initial interview, ask the prospective employer about the work schedule. Depending on your personal circumstances, you may not be able to pull off certain shifts. If that is the case, make sure you communicate this clearly to the employer. Generally, you will find employers willing to make arrangements to accommodate employees, especially if they see potential in them.

Most employers have at-will employment policies. This means that the employer or employee can terminate the employment at any time. In general, employers are required to provide probable cause to terminate employment, whereas employees don't. Most companies have trial periods in place that, in general, are about ninety days. Employers will closely monitor the new hire's performance during the trial period.

Most part-time positions, generally thirty-two hours or less, don't come with benefits. Usually, they are considered a supplemental source of income or can be looked at as an opportunity to pave your way into a full-time position with your dream company.

Here in the States, it's common to see entry-level positions paid on an hourly basis and management positions at a fixed salary. Back in Uzbekistan, the notion of paying by the hour does not exist as of writing this book. Folks are either paid a fixed monthly salary or project-based.

Don't get thrown off if you are offered hourly pay, especially when you are starting out. To figure out your monthly salary, multiply the hourly sum by 2,080 (the average of how many hours a full-time person works per year) and divide it by 12.

Payments are usually made weekly or biweekly on specific days outlined by your employer. Employers generally hold the deposit, and typically, it's one or two weeks' worth of payment. Therefore, as a new employee, expect to wait a bit longer for your first paycheck. The payment terms and schedule will be outlined in the employee handbook, yet make sure you ask about it during the interview.

Regardless of whether you are a full-time or a part-time employee, make sure you dress in a manner that is appropriate to the job you have taken. This doesn't just mean wearing nice clothes, but also clothes that are suitable for the environment you find yourself in. A bank manager who is wearing jeans and a t-shirt will not be taken seriously.

It's also important to stay focused, work hard at everything you do, and maintain healthy relationships with your employers and coworkers, even at only temporary jobs. You never know when you might find yourself needing to cross back over a bridge that you hastily burned. Former employers and coworkers can make for an excellent network when it comes to acquiring new opportunities, so nurture your relationships accordingly.

It's also worth mentioning that you don't have to do everything that is asked of you. Sometimes, employers assign more work than is manageable. If you feel that you don't have enough time to handle all of the tasks you have been given, it is okay to bring this up politely to your boss(es).

Much of the time, your employer will be happy to help you find a way to make your schedule a little more comfortable. Advancement in the workplace is usually contingent on performance. To that end, simply showing up every day and giving it everything you have may be enough to get noticed. That means avoiding sick days whenever you can work without exposing others to your illness.

It also means taking care of yourself so that you can work every day. Avoid late nights and partying throughout the workweek. Remember that your employer counts on your attendance and performance on your next scheduled workday.

Don't be afraid to take on more responsibilities. Promotions and raises will come when you are able to show your employer that you are capable of taking on additional responsibilities while delivering on your promises. The American system generally rewards people for working harder and having an ambitious attitude. This has its complexities, like anything, but generally, this kind of approach will be rewarded.

Communication skills will also help set you apart from your coworkers. Most highly successful people aren't just intelligent and driven; they are also great at working with others, influencing the people around them to work toward the same goal.

Keep in mind that courtesy doesn't end just because you've decided your current job is no longer for you. If you must quit, be sure to give at least two weeks' advance notice.

This will help your existing employer at least start looking for your replacement. As an employer myself, I can tell you that your new boss will probably be delighted to hear that you can't start for two weeks if the reason behind it is that you need to give your previous employer a heads-up.

Don't hesitate to speak your mind. America encourages free and creative thinking. Good ideas are always welcome, especially at your place of work. They may even have the benefit of impacting your career positively. Having said that, be mindful of your rank; you can't just speak your mind freely whenever you feel like it. In many settings, you need to be respectful.

Try to live by a standard that will provide a good life. Keep the good relationships and end the bad. Break harmful habits that could inhibit you at work or home. Be on time, work hard, be polite, and assume only the responsibilities you can handle. In short, model behaviors that reflect the outcomes you hope to achieve. Internalize this so that it informs not just your actions but also your dress, posture, and words.

HOW TO LOOK FOR EMPLOYMENT

In America, finding work is relatively easy if you genuinely want a job. Below you will find some tips on how to find a job:

- Ask your friends, family, and even neighbors.
- Use online resources such as Facebook Jobs *(www.facebook.com)*, Indeed *(www.indeed.com)*, ZipRecruiter *(www.ziprecruiter.com)*, Monster *(www.monster.com)*, LinkedIn *(www.linkedin.com)* etc.

- Check the local newspaper's jobs section. Your local grocery store may also have a bulletin board displaying this section.

- Look up and apply with staffing or temporary employment agencies near your location.

- Find businesses that fit your criteria, walk in, and ask to fill out an application. Going in person is a great way to stand out. Although it is worth mentioning that many companies only have online application processes now. Don't try to cover big territory in one day alone. Break it down into smaller chunks. You need to look fresh when walking into the businesses to introduce yourself because, at times, you could be handing your resume to the decision-maker. Stay optimistic, energized, and hydrated, you don't want to get discouraged by a grinding process. Keep in mind that each completed application and hand-delivered resume is taking you closer to your ideal job.

Don't get discouraged by rejections either. Remember, each "No" will bring you closer to "Yes." Keep in mind that all you need to succeed is that one right opportunity.

The most important thing to realize is that America has over thirty million small businesses[17] alone, not to mention

---

[17] "Frequently Asked Questions About Small Business, 2020 - SBA." https://cdn.advocacy.sba.gov/wp-content/uploads/2020/11/05122043/Small-Business-FAQ-2020.pdf. Accessed 4 Mar. 2022.

medium and large businesses. There is always someone looking for the right candidate.

Make sure your resume stands out when you apply. If you need help creating or polishing your resume before applying there is plenty of qualified talent on freelancer websites such as Upwork *(www.upwork.com)*, and Fiverr *(www.fiverr.com)*. Dress to impress at an interview. Ask questions. Show your employer why and how you can contribute to the success of the organization.

Although how much the job will pay you is an essential question, there is an even more critical question to be asked while determining which employer to work for. It's one you ask yourself: "What am I becoming?"

Bet on an employer who is willing to invest in you. Work for a company where your growth potential is not limited.

Once, I took a $3.75 per hour job parking cars versus a $10 per hour job serving banquets. The main reason for my decision was that I saw more significant growth potential in parking cars because it would open a door to be promoted to the front desk. I was correct, as eventually, the valet job led to the front desk, where I had access to learn computer technologies and apply for different office positions.

I later rejected the supervisor position at the hotel in favor of working for a small home improvement and development company as an office manager. The office manager role prepared me for what was about to come next: starting my own business!

I am very happy that I made those moves. I see way too many entrepreneurs ending up as glorified employees in their own companies simply because they have not been armed with the knowledge and experience I had gained from my office manager position. Instead of managing the work and employees, business owners end up doing the work themselves. As a business owner, your goal should be to work ON it, not IN it.

As you can see from my story, it's more important to invest in your future by asking the right question: "Who am I becoming at this job?" instead of focusing on your immediate pay.

It is noteworthy to mention that the U.S. has several laws that forbid employers from discriminating against those looking for a job and protect employees against retaliation and other forms of discrimination.

Employers can't discriminate based on race, religion, country of origin, color, sex, pregnancy, age, or disability.

For more information about these protections, visit the U.S. Equal Employment Opportunity Commission website at *www.eeoc.gov* or call 1.800.669.4000.

WORKING FOR YOURSELF

My fellow immigrant friends, I am excited you have made it to this stage. All these years, you have overcome obstacles, worked faithfully for your employer, and improved your skills and learning.

Now may be the right time to start thinking about working for yourself. Why?

As Farrah Gray said, "Build your own dreams, or someone else will hire you to build theirs."

America is truly the land of opportunity! I remember being employed and hearing this phrase so many times that it started sounding like a cliché.

Now, after all these years of working for myself, I can say that I fully understand the meaning behind those words. This *is* the land of opportunity!

You can succeed at any trade or occupation you choose. The money is here, the innovation is here, the consumers are here.

Did you know that the U.S. government itself is the largest purchaser of services and goods in the world? Yes! The government!

You can sell your goods and services not only to consumers and businesses but also to the U.S. government itself! If you think about it, your chances of success skyrocket just by being strategic and landing the government as a client. Just one perfect client, such as the government, can set you financially free.

And the best news is that this is not rocket science. The U.S. government solicits its contract opportunities openly so that any qualifying companies can bid.

HOW TO CHOOSE YOUR BUSINESS

The good news is that you can pick what you are good at and what you love and then turn it into a business. The marketplace is vast, and there is a demand for everything!

Regardless of what you decide to do, as long as you are creative, ethical, eager to learn, and willing to take action, you will most likely succeed. The good news is that you don't even have to be the finest or smartest at what you do, just know the trade 10% better than your target audience/ clientele and love it. Enter the process with a willingness to learn and grow, and with a bit of luck, consistency, and creativity, you will do just fine.

When I was considering starting a company, I debated between offering IT consulting services or cleaning services.

After analyzing the consulting industry, I discovered that the industry was packed with extremely smart people. Being a tad better than the smartest people is really hard.

Since I am not that gifted, I decided to invest in cleaning services after clearly laying out my options and capabilities. I thought most cleaning industry people possess average business savvy and are not the proverbial rocket scientists. This meant that to succeed, I only had to be better than average.

That's how I got locked into the cleaning industry.

COMFORT ZONE

As Neale Donald Walsch said, "Life begins at the end of your comfort zone."

Have you ever examined how lobsters grow?

Lobsters are soft animals that live inside of a hard shell. That shell doesn't expand. As lobsters grow, their shells become uncomfortable. The only way for them to grow is to molt and grow a new shell. When they drop their shell, they become extremely vulnerable to predators. Yet, if they don't, they won't grow.

Lobsters shed their shells (exiting their comfort zone) and hide in the rocks (exposing themselves to the threat of being found by a predator) while they grow new shells. And they do this several times throughout their life cycle.

They take great risk in opting for growth, and, in turn, they are rewarded with stronger, bigger bodies.

The moral of the story is that change is full of unknowns. Anything unknown is scary. And our 40,000-year-old brains are wired to keep us alive by keeping us outside of harm's way. If we listen to our brains, we will never grow. To grow, we must find the courage to act and step out of our comfort zone.

Courage is not acting because you feel no fear, it's acting in spite of it!

Many of us are afraid to start working for ourselves because of the feeling of insecurity that comes with the unknown. We think that our employer "guarantees" our paychecks, thus we are able to meet our financial obligations. I also understand that the older we get, the more baggage we carry. Thus, taking risks becomes even riskier.

At the time of writing, I have been working for myself for over fourteen years. I can tell you that working for myself is more secure than working for an employer. Even if I try and fail, I will fail because of my own mistakes, not because of some manager. When working for someone else, your performance is not the only factor that determines success. You could do your job perfectly; it won't matter if the business fails or conducts layoffs for some strategic reason outside your control.

Starting your own business is a little like learning to speak a new language. In the beginning, you will be uncomfortable, but as time passes and your skills advance, it will become second nature.

In my case, I was somewhat forced to resign. I had been faithfully working with my last employer for over three years. The company was growing, and the owners decided to introduce a new position: controller.

The controller and I didn't start things off right for some reason. He regularly portrayed me in a negative light in front of the company owners, and I ultimately left to salvage the relationships I still had there.

Ironically, the controller was fired six months after my departure. To this day, I have kept a good relationship with both of my previous employers. I still benefit from their wisdom and friendship.

Having said that, the transition was scary. I had to work a lot of hours. I then figured out how Google's algorithm was working and was able to build Interworld Cleaning online, relying on Joomla *(www.joomla.com)*, a free and open-sourced content management system.

Initially, I would take orders, negotiate, and run the business during the mornings. In the early afternoons, I would schedule cleaning jobs and do them myself or with the help of friends and family. I would work more on the website and online presence in the evenings.

In a short amount of time, I faced a challenge as my office hours started to overlap with my cleaning hours. That's when I decided to bring in help. In the beginning, I started outsourcing cleaning services, then I started outsourcing website-building services, then phone-answering services, and from there, growth began.

I must admit that one of the biggest things I had to learn was how to delegate control.

If you have difficulty ceding control, the risk of micro-managing is real. To avoid this, think of becoming a teacher and mentor who encourages your protégée to take charge and make decisions. In time, you will find that the empowerment and autonomy you have offered have helped your business and provided another person with invaluable job skills.

Why should you invest in yourself? Because no one else will pay you what you are really worth. The ultimate goal is to stop trading your time for money.

Make alliances with those you respect and want to emulate. Create partnerships; learn from them. Strive to create a win-win situation.

I have seen a common mistake: endless waiting. Waiting until everything is known, until the conditions are right, until problems are settled, until money/partners/location/etc.

The truth is, conditions are never right and you will never know everything; there will always be questions and uncertainties. You are only procrastinating and postponing. If you keep waiting for the perfect moment, I am afraid you will be waiting forever.

The good news is you don't have to know everything about that particular business. Industries evolve, and it's almost impossible to catch up with all the changes and innovation. You are good to go if you feel you have the necessary knowledge to get started, are passionate about it, and willing to learn and adapt. Of course, depending on your industry, ensure you have all the required certifications and licenses. Be determined, set challenging goals, and start taking action. Partners, money, connections, and anything else you wish, will come along the way.

Join groups, attend events, get involved with your community, and make friends with like-minded people. Be mindful, be strategic. Remember: Continuous forward motion over waiting until it's perfect will usually get you better results.

Remember the lobsters, and don't hesitate to step out of your comfort zone!

THE MAIN FOUR WAYS TO EARN

As we already know, there are mainly four ways to earn money:

1. Employment - The more you work, the more you make, usually, or so we think. Generally, this serves as an entry point for most of us. The problem is that you are limited to your own time. When you stop working, you stop making money. The older you get, the less active you become, and the less time you will be able to work/earn. In this case, your earning capabilities are directly correlated to the hours you are able to put in regardless of your profession.

2. Becoming part of a pyramid - It's usually a scam where folks at the bottom work to enrich the folks at the top. You work hard to sell tangible or intangible

products, you make commissions, your boss makes a commission, and his/her boss makes a commission, etc. The folks at the very bottom carry those at the top, e.g., selling recurring insurance policies or beauty line products. Some even require your "skin in the game" and will ask you to buy the "very first batch." In my opinion, those are even worse. Not only are you losing your time and potential opportunity, but you're also losing your hard-earned money.

3. Starting your own business - usually by offering goods and/or services. This option may seem most uncertain when you are starting out. Especially when you look into stats of how many businesses fail; the numbers may freak you out. However, this is how millionaires and billionaires are made. Focus on solving someone else's problem. One of my mentors, Mr. Jimmy Rhee, says, solve a problem for millions, and you are a millionaire, solve it for billions, and you are a billionaire.

4. Passive income - This is typically generated by investing large amounts of funds into a business (sometimes risky yet promising start-ups), acquiring real estate/stocks/crypto, and/or trademarking intellectual capital such as inventions/books/online courses. In most cases, this approach requires a greater amount of money, specialized in-depth knowledge, and/or connections to get into.

In my opinion, you have the most control over your destiny in the third scenario. Once you build up enough capital, connections, in-depth knowledge, and/or experience, you can start investing in Scenario 4.

With any business, you will face challenges. The question is not IF, the question is WHEN. In general, it takes years to become an expert. Therefore, be very selective with your energy and resources. Stay focused and stick to your goal.

In *Outliers*, Malcolm Gladwell breaks down the 10,000-hour rule very nicely.

Successful people take the necessary time to evaluate as many options as they can before reaching a decision. Yet once a decision has been made, they stick with it and don't change their minds easily.

For example, the legendary Henry Ford is known for his refusal to change course on Model T development even after burning all the money he received from his initial investors.

Thomas Edison continued working on the light bulb despite his many failures. When asked about it, he said, "I have not failed. I've just found 10,000 ways that won't work."

Leverage your immigrant mentality. Remember, it's not your weakness, it's your strength.

As Tony Robbins said, "Success leaves clues." See what other successful people are doing and mimic it.

Perseverance is a common attribute among successful entrepreneurs. Go in knowing the road will be difficult. Rise to the occasion with determination and agility, and you will do just fine.

Once you pick your field, stay laser-focused and always promote healthy and ethical business practices.

After all, what goes around comes around. If you are unethical, your employees will see that and think it's normal and most likely will behave dishonestly toward you. Further, you could find yourself surrounded by similarly unethical people.

ALWAYS PROTECT YOUR CONFIDENCE

Protecting your confidence at all times should be one of your top priorities—especially while running your business. Be mindful of those who whisper in your ears day in and day out. Be careful even with the podcasts and audiobooks you listen to. Feed your brain with positive affirmations and knowledge that will only make you stronger and better and strengthen your confidence daily.

On an intuitive level, humans, like animals, can sense the vibrations that the other party is projecting. The doe doesn't teach its fawn not to approach wolves, still, fawns avoid wolves like fire. Confident people generally don't associate themselves with insecure people; successful doesn't hang out with unsuccessful.

Here are some examples of confidence-threatening negativity: "You are an immigrant in this country, and that's why you can't be/do/achieve X"; "You are not good enough"; "You were not born into a wealthy family"; "You have never studied X/you have no experience in X, and therefore you are doomed to failure"; "You have an accent, and that's why you will never achieve X"; "You will never earn more than what you are earning right now"; "There is no such thing as work-life balance in this world."

My advice: Stay away from negative, self-limiting beliefs/people.

I don't even listen to much daily news. Most of the time, the media shows tragic events and horror stories.

Since most of the news is tragic and I can't make it better, I don't give it space in my head.

I am not suggesting to become oblivious. By all means, pay attention to what is happening in the world around you, and understand it. But don't let this understanding come at the cost of your good mood, ambition, or confidence.

NAMING YOUR COMPANY

Once you determine what type of services or products you want to offer, the next step, and one of the hardest, is naming your business.

Many make the mistake of naming their company after themselves.

This is when our ego comes to play. Although our name is the sweetest sound to us, remember, those looking for your services won't know it. To them, it makes no difference.

Of course, once you gain fame and glory and have made a name for yourself, you can name your next company after yourself or even "rent" your name to earn passive income in the same way as Calvin Klein, Tommy Hilfiger, Gucci, etc.

But for now, think of a catchy, smart name that clearly relates your services/products, and ideally your values, to your potential clients.

For example, instead of Maria's Services, consider naming your company Green Home Cleaning Services.

The company's name identifies its industry (residential cleaning services) and by what principles it abides (environmental responsibility).

Russians have a saying that translates to something along the following lines of "As you name the ship so that it will sail." In my experience, this saying has some truth to that. Take your time when naming your company.

Full disclosure: I wanted to call my cleaning company Shukurov's Cleaning Company. Looking back now, I am so happy I went with Interworld Cleaning instead.

MOST COMMON BUSINESS ENTITY TYPES

- **Sole Proprietorships** - Also known as the sole trader or individual entrepreneurship or proprietorship, this is a type of enterprise that is owned and run by one person and in which there is no legal distinction between the owner and the business entity.

- **Limited Liability Corporations** (LLCs) - This enterprise blends elements of partnership and corporate structures. The primary characteristic an LLC shares with a corporation is limited liability, and the primary characteristic it shares with a partnership is the availability of pass-through income taxation. It is often more flexible than a corporation, and it is well-suited for companies with a single owner.

- **Business Corporation** - Shareholders own the company, and directors are elected by the shareholders who govern the company. In general, it provides more protection, i.e., a "corporate veil."

C Corp - Income tax is taxed separately from its owners.
S Corp - Income, losses, and deductions pass through shareholders.

- **Partnerships** - This is the most basic type of structure for two or more people owning a business. Liabilities and rights and duties are divided equally between partners unless it is specified otherwise.

- **Nonprofits** - These are organizations that use surplus revenues to achieve their goals rather than distributing them as profit or dividends. From a tax filing perspective they are more complex.

An LLC is the most common form of business entity due to the healthier balance between liability, taxation, and the amount of work required.

EMPLOYER IDENTIFICATION NUMBER (EIN)

Once you have your company's name, follow your state's registration requirements. After that, you will need to apply for an EIN with the IRS.

Each person has their own SSN so each company will have its own EIN. EINs are free. Here is the link to apply with the IRS: *www.irs.gov/businesses/small-businesses-self-employed/apply-for-an-employer-identification-number-ein-online.*

If you are a sole proprietor or a single-member LLC without employees, you may operate your business under your SSN. However, I have never liked the notion of giving away my SSN; therefore, I prefer to work under an EIN. Besides, obtaining an EIN doesn't cost anything, so why not?

BANK ACCOUNTS

After registering your company and acquiring an EIN, the next step is to set up your banking. As referenced in the Personal Finance chapter, plenty of financial institutions will be willing to work with you.

In the States, banks and bankers are here to serve us and compete for our business. It appeared completely the opposite in Uzbekistan, the bankers seemed to be a part of the so-called "prestige group." Therefore, it took me a while to flip my viewpoint about the entire sector. I now realize that banks need us the same way we need our customers.

Opening a business bank account is fairly simple, you will need to present the following documents:

1. EIN, if you haven't filed for it, then SSN should suffice.

2. Personal identification, e.g., a driver's license, passport, green card.

3. Business details, e.g., business name, address, trade name if applicable.

4. Business organizing documents filed with a state, e.g., registration certificate, articles of organization/incorporation, operating agreement, business license, bylaws.

5. Deposit, the minimum required amount, which will vary by bank.

The main thing to watch out for is the fees. Make sure you are thoroughly familiar with the bank's fees structure.

It feels like some banks assess fees for every little thing. Stay away from those.

Another important attribute for me is whether I get a personal banker assigned or not. Having a direct point of contact will come in handy as you face challenges growing your business. Also, check out the bank's operating hours and number of locations within your area.

Don't rush with opening your corporate bank account. Perform your due diligence. Shop around to compare rates. Different financial institutions offer different perks, so don't be afraid to negotiate. Best case, you will get slightly better terms established for your company.

Depending on your industry, some things may be more important than others for you. For example, if you are in real estate, you will often use wire services. Perhaps you can negotiate a reduced fee for those wire transactions. In construction, you may need to void issued checks regularly, so you may wish to negotiate along those lines.

About a decade after I started Interworld Cleaning, I was pleasantly surprised to have representatives from different prestigious financial institutions in our office trying to sell their services (while offering additional perks) after we decided to switch banks. .

Most banks are either a member of the Federal Deposit Insurance Corporation or FDIC (*www.fdic.gov*) or insured by the National Credit Union Administration or NCUS (*www.ncua.gov*). Your funds in those banks are protected for up to $250,000.

Be mindful of your spending and try not to process a payment over what you actually have in your bank. This is a sure way to incur overdraft fees, and in some cases, banks will decline the charge. Repeatedly doing so will accumulate unnecessary costs and may negatively affect your credit score.

BUSINESS CREDIT CARDS

You will also need a business credit card. Like an individual, businesses must establish their creditworthiness. It's best to establish your business credit history as quickly as possible. In time, your business will qualify for purchases without your (the owner's) personal guarantee. This means your buying power will go up while risks go down.

Use the same approach as with banking, shop for credit cards. Pursue the ones that offer the most perks and/or are best suited to your circumstances, don't overspend, and pay the balance off at the end of each month.

Perks include but are not limited to cash back rewards, points redeemable for flights/travel/lodging, extended warranty for a purchased product, concierge service, and additional discounts.

FORGING PARTNERSHIPS

Create partnerships and joint ventures whenever possible. Be strategic with choosing your business partner. Don't just go with your closest friend. Remember, during the tenure of your partnership, your friendship (if you end up going with a friend) will be tested. Some friendships don't survive this test. Therefore, be mindful of who you partner with.

Make sure your business partner complements your skills to create a powerful union without weak links.

For example, if you are good in the front office, let's say at SAM (sales and marketing), pick a partner who brings strong back-office skills, e.g., accounting and bookkeeping.

Don't be greedy either. Splitting profits down the middle is not a bad thing. Keep in mind that, at the same time, you are splitting liabilities as well, i.e., half the risk, half the work, half the investments, etc. Abundance is in abundance; there is more than enough for all.

When you join forces, a "Mastermind" is born. You reduce your workload and risk, all while increasing your chances of hitting your target sooner. With the right partner, your journey will be slightly more comfortable, and you will have someone to huddle and brainstorm with when winter arrives.

ESSENTIAL PLAYERS TO HAVE ON YOUR TEAM

Have the following players on your team, build relationships, and become friends with them:

- Lawyers (In our case, on top of having a great business/criminal lawyer, we also need to have an immigration lawyer on our side.)
- Accountants
- Insurance agents
- Bankers and fiduciaries

Make sure they are getting fairly compensated for the work they do for you. The right team of professionals will look out for your best interests and will always be protecting you.

I am happy to report that I was able to forge strong friendships with these professionals and even entered into business partnerships with some of them.

I am not saying you should try to get close to every attorney you interact with. Trust me, when you are intentional and genuine, you will find the people from these fields with whom you will be able to align and bond long-lasting, mutually beneficial relationships.

OUTSOURCING

No person can build an empire on their own. Nor will one person know it all. You need to learn your strengths and weaknesses. Focus on developing your strengths and learn how to outsource (delegate) your weaknesses.

I believe strongly in the benefits of outsourcing. You can't be the best at everything, and in trying to acquire new skills, you take yourself away from your other responsibilities. Self-improvement is, of course, a good thing, but at a certain point, you must draw a line between what you can do and what you should allow others to do for you.

Use sites such as Upwork and Fiverr to find freelancers who complement you. As an example, even to write this book, I am using the help of a freelancer because English is not my first language.

Of course, I could spend more time learning and perfecting my English and skip the freelancer's help altogether. Yet had I done so, I would be doing a disservice to myself and to my readers. This book would have taken much longer to write and may never have been completed at all.

BUSTING MYTHS

Myth# 1 - Working hard will make you rich, yes?

How many people can you point out who have worked hard their entire life and achieved true wealth and abundance? The goal should be to work smart, not hard. The "work hard, and you will be rich" myth is inaccurate. The successful are constantly seeking the most innovative ways to multiply their income.

The ultimate goal is to work on what you find fulfilling while still making enough money to maintain your lifestyle. Scratch "work hard" from your vocabulary and replace it with "work smart."

Myth# 2 - Everyone has 24 hours in a day, right?

I would like you to challenge this perception. Think about the wealthiest people on the planet. Somehow, they have learned how to accomplish more in the same twenty-four hours that we are all given.

How? By hiring help, delegating work, subcontracting out, outsourcing responsibilities, and asking and/or incentivizing others to work for them or with them.

Myth# 3 – No one can be in two places at the same time, correct?

Not true. The same successful folks can do multiple things simultaneously, which means they have learned how to be in multiple places at once. No, this is not science fiction.

Let me explain; a business owner has people working for him/her in different positions simultaneously: accounting, sales, and marketing, manufacturing, collections, project management, procurement, etc.

In a manner of speaking, the owner has learned how to be in multiple places at the same time doing numerous things.

Without the assistance of others, you truly are bound by the laws of space and time. Take the example of a masseuse. People in this profession can make good money, but only when they are with a client. The moment they take a break or rest, their earning power drops to zero. However, someone who owns a massage parlor can continue making money even when they are not personally on the premises.

Also, the older you get, the more fatigue you will feel, which means the less you will be able to work physically.

The ultimate goal of working for yourself is to figure out how to make money when you are sleeping, how to make money when you are sick, how to make money on vacation, and how to make money when you retire.

In other words, the goal is to stop exchanging your time for money. And this can be achieved by creating a business that can work without you. Create systems and procedures, hire folks, and motivate and inspire others to work toward the same goal. A true abundance can be achieved by working with a dedicated team toward the same goal as opposed to pulling the entire weight on your own.

"Never believe that a few caring people can't change the world. For, indeed, that's all who ever have." - Margaret Mead

Be brave, and move forward. The world needs what you have to offer. The world needs you. No one will pay you what you deserve except yourself. Don't let limiting beliefs hold you back.

I have no doubt that there will be obstacles, but the sooner you embark on this exciting journey, the sooner you will overcome them, and the sooner you will start enjoying the joy and freedom of working for yourself.

"Our dreams come true if we have the power to pursue them" - Walt Disney.

Congratulations on finishing Chapter 10!

Use the following questions to help you reflect on the chapter you just read.

1. Are you willing to step outside your comfort zone to pursue new career opportunities?

2. Does your business concept harmonize with your passion, skills, and future aspirations?

3. Who will be pivotal to your business success and how do you plan to cultivate these relationships?

Your progress so far   77%

10/13

CHAPTER 11
PUBLIC SERVICE & POLITICAL AMBITIONS

Although this is a short chapter, it carries a very important message. If you have come this far and your calling now is to serve in public office, I applaud you.

The beauty of this country is you can become almost anyone you would like to become. I am using the word "almost" because there are two public positions you can't occupy unless you are born in the United States.

The President and Vice President's offices require candidates to be naturally born citizens at least thirty-five years of age.

The good news is that any other political position below those two can be achieved. For example, immigrants can be elected to the Senate if they have been citizens for nine years or be elected to the House if they have been citizens for seven years. To become governor, you must only have been a citizen for five years.

In other words, immigrants interested in seeking elected office have many options available to them. Indeed, there are even advantages to being an immigrant. Coming from another country with a unique culture and political system, we have a range of experiences that other candidates might not have.

To that end, our background makes us more valuable in contributing to the U.S.'s political landscape. There are many immigrant politicians who achieved their desired results by following their passion and deciding to serve the nation.

Congratulations on finishing Chapter 11!

Use the following questions to help you reflect on the chapter you just read.

1. In your view, which U.S. president, past or present, has had the most significant influence on your country?

2. Name notable immigrants from foreign countries who rose to prominence in the U.S., like Arnold Schwarzenegger.

3. When contrasting the U.S. federal democratic republic with your home country's governance, what significant differences do you notice?

Your progress so far   85%

11/13

CHAPTER 12

GIVING BACK TO THE COMMUNITY & MAKING AN IMPACT

Do you know what feels better than receiving gifts? Giving them.

I believe one can't achieve complete harmony and emotional satisfaction until one starts giving back. Giving back can be in many forms. You will feel most satisfied when the action is sincere and expect nothing in return. In this chapter, we will discuss how you, as an immigrant, can give back to this country and the Planet Earth.

Let's be frank, we all came here in pursuit of a better opportunity and better life. For the majority of us, if the conditions were favorable in our countries, we wouldn't have left everyone we knew to relocate to the United States.

This country has welcomed us, gave us shelter, opportunities, and fair treatment. The least we can do is pull our own weight by working, paying taxes, and giving back to the communities we live and work in. Remember, prosperity in this country is a benefit to everyone, from the people we help, to the children we may one day bring into the world.

There are many ways to give back. You could create jobs, contribute to innovation, volunteer, donate money to charitable causes, and much more. Indeed, the number of ways you can improve the community is often limited only by your imagination and time limitations.

Do your best to pay it forward, as I have done. Help out other immigrants; teach them basics, help them find lodging and employment, and guide them to their success.

A few Americans stigmatize immigrants by thinking we are here to break laws, steal their jobs, and other inaccurate, fear-inducing assumptions. By working smart and ethically, we can change these harmful mindsets. America is a nation built by immigrants. Let's reignite the feeling!

Together we are stronger. Stand united! Join organizations that match your values and take on leadership roles. This will also help you to meet other like-minded people and expand your reach.

SUSTAINABILITY & RESPONSIBILITY

While talking about giving back and making a positive impact, let's not forget that there is something greater than us, our families, and the countries. It's our mother planet—Earth.

Our why for immigrating to the States will vary for each of us: harsh economic conditions, gang violence, unstable government, oppression of free will, uninhabitable conditions, and everything in between. Only you know the true reason why you decided to make this leap. Whatever that thing or combination of those things, you may have found it to be beyond repair. Luckily for us, we were able to find a better country to relocate to.

Having said that, we must realize that we all have only one planet to share. If we mess up the planet beyond repair, there is no other planet for us to immigrate to—end of the story.

I, and unfortunately, all of the people of Central Asia, know firsthand about the consequences of a man-made ecological catastrophe: the desiccation of the Aral Sea, formerly the world's fourth-largest lake in the area. The leading cause is the Soviet-era diversion of water inflow for irrigation purposes, primarily cotton plantations.

Nowadays, even in Tashkent, the capital of Uzbekistan, previously known for its clean, crisp, and humid air full of trees and shade, some winters go without snow, extreme heat waves, sand storms, and scarcity of drinking water. The climate is becoming more similar to those countries located close to deserts.

Tragically, it's not just Tashkent but the entire region, including all surrounding countries around, what used to be, the magnificent Aral Sea.

We must wake up and realize there is no other planet to move into if we mess up this one. Each of us must play our part in preserving this planet for future generations. Luckily, it's not too difficult and within our control.

Whenever possible, follow the 5 R principles in the order they are listed below:

1. Refuse - Say NO to plastic, wasteful/unnecessary purchases/shopping, and products that harm the environment.

2. Reduce - Only purchase things you need and donate the rest so others can benefit from it.

3. Reuse - Reuse any item you can; it will save the need to produce new things.

4. Repurpose - Before trashing items, consider whether they can be used in another way.

5. Recycle - If all of the above fails, then recycle.

Let's leave this planet to our future generations in better shape than we inherited it.

Congratulations on finishing Chapter 12!

Use the following questions to help you reflect on the chapter you just read.

1. How can you contribute to sustainability and responsibility in your community?

2. How can your distinct strengths be utilized to create a positive influence on others?

3. How will you engage in community initiatives and actively contribute back?

Your progress so far — 92%

12/13

CHAPTER 13
DON'T FORGET YOUR HERITAGE, LANGUAGE, & CULTURE

My fellow immigrants, my friends, you, and I have now come to the final chapter. It has truly been an honor and a privilege. And here it seems appropriate to bring your attention back to your roots and heritage. Turn the focus wheel on those binoculars so we can clearly see the true source of our success and stamina, regardless of how painful our pasts may have been.

THE PRICE WE ALL PAY

To obtain something, one must give something in return. To have a fit body, you need to work out and eat healthy. To pick up that latest phone, you have to have money to pay for it. To purchase a house, you should have at least the required minimums (credit score, down payment, sources of income). To become successful, you must be willing to put in countless hours and take risks.

As immigrants, most of us have made a conscious decision to move to the States to pursue something better.

Others, such as Dreamers protected by DACA (the Deferred Action on Childhood Arrivals program) may have been brought in involuntarily or escaped violence and instabilities in their home countries. Regardless of the reasoning, most of us thought it would be better for us and/or our loved ones to be here than there.

This change comes with a perhaps not-so-obvious price tag.

After arriving in the States, I couldn't see my parents, friends, and family for the first five-and-a-half years. And I consider my case mild compared to other examples I have witnessed.

I have seen kids growing up without their mom and/or dad, children unable to bury their parents, long-distance marriages crash, grandparents unable to witness the birth of their grandchildren, lifelong friends grow apart, and the list goes on and on.

Yes, I still believe that America is the best country to live in. I included this not to freak you out but to ensure that you are consciously aware while making this monumental decision.

In my case, the price I paid for what I got in return was worth it. As long as you feel the same, then you are doing well.

INCREASING ODDS IN OUR FAVOR

In our home, we were quite firm about speaking only the native (Uzbek) language, and on the TV, we only played Russian programs. No English language was used inside the house except when guests arrived. This allowed our oldest to pick up the Uzbek and Russian languages. The second one followed suit. Now, both of our daughters are fluent in Uzbek, Russian, and English!

It's common for second-generation immigrants to lose their native language altogether. Indeed, some children born here even begin to feel ashamed of their native culture.

It's sad that this happens, yet parents have the power to influence their children's perspective on their heritage and culture. Consider developing and encouraging a multicultural atmosphere in your house. By implementing a "no English beyond this door" policy in our homes, we can help our kids preserve our native languages.

Children certainly have the bandwidth to appreciate their native culture while still enjoying an entirely authentic American experience.

Since nothing is guaranteed in this life (except death and taxes), the best we can do is increase the odds in our favor. After all, knowing more languages and being exposed to our cultures will provide our children with benefits and advantages they will eventually appreciate. By giving a gift of a second language, we are supercharging our kids and increasing their chances of being more successful in this life.

Don't stop with just the language; take the best from our cultures, such as respect for the elderly, deeply rooted love for our families and the planet, and beautiful traditions/heritage and leave out the bad such as bribery, corruption, and greed.

Imagine an army of immigrant wunderkinders growing up and becoming contributing members of this country.

Think of the tremendous things they could do for America and the world, including our home countries.

Picture a day when immigrants moving into a neighborhood becomes a sign of improvement because it is understood that we will get involved and contribute.

This is precisely how we break stereotypes.

PARTING WORDS & ADVICE

Some call the U.S. a melting pot, a collection of cultures coming together to form America. I prefer the analogy of a salad bar. We don't melt, we mingle, with each culture bringing its own flavor to the table.

Remember, you are who you are because of your heritage and your past. Embrace it.

Now go ahead, and make a difference! As Jeff Bezos said, "In the end, we are our choices. Build yourself a great story."

Carry on my immigrant friends, your new life awaits....

Congratulations on finishing Chapter 13!

Use the following questions to help you reflect on the chapter you just read.

1. What holds a special place in your heart from your home country, something you'll miss when you leave? How do you plan to fill that void or find something similar in the U.S.?

2. Which cultural tradition or element from your homeland will you maintain regardless you settle? How do you intend to sustain it in your new environment?

3. Among the diverse U.S. cultures, is there one that especially intrigues you and sparks your excitement to explore?

Your progress so far.. Good job!   100%

13/13

APPENDIX

RECOMMENDED READING

1. *The Richest Man in Babylon* - George S. Clason --- Learn how to achieve an almost predictable path to a comfortable retirement. Make your money work for you.

2. *Think Big and Grow Rich* - Napoleon Hill --- Read this book to unlock a secret key to a massive impact and wealth.

3. *Miracle Morning Millionaires* - Hal Elrod, David Osborn, Honoree Corder --- Find out how to structure your morning to set yourself on a winning path.

4. *Never Split the Difference: Negotiating As If Your Life Depended On It* - Chris Voss --- Uncover secrets of human psychology to learn how to effectively negotiate with those around you.

5. *Atomic Habits* - James Clear --- Discover the power of small habits that will eventually lead you to great success.

6. *The Top 5 Regrets of the Dying* - Bronnie Ware --- In the end, what makes life worth living? Some of the answers lay in this book.

7. *Essentialism: The Disciplined Pursuit of Less* - Greg McKeown --- Simplify your life, and find out how the pursuit of less but better can bring you more of what you want.

8. *Outliers: The Story of Success* - Malcolm Gladwell --- Find out why some turn out to be more successful than others and reciprocate their success, so you can provide a competitive edge to your children.

9. *The 5 Love Languages: The Secret to Love that Lasts* - Gary Chapman --- Express your feelings and show love and gratitude to those you care about in their language.

10. *Limitless: Upgrade Your Brain, Learn Anything Faster, and Unlock Your Exceptional Life* - Jim Kwik --- Upgrade your learning skills to become truly unstoppable.

11. *Simplicity Parenting: Using the Extraordinary Power of Less to Raise Calmer, Happier, and More Secure Kids* - Kim John Payne --- Discover how to create more space for your children so you can promote their creativity and growth without robbing them of their childhood.

12. *Go for No! Yes Is the Destination, No Is How You Get There* - Richard Fenton, Andrea Waltz --- Need to boost your sales? Read this book to learn quick techniques that can increase your closing ratio.

13. *The 7 Habits of Highly Effective People* - Stephen R. Covey --- Find out what successful people do, so you can, too, become a success.

14. *Meditations; A New Translation* - Marcus Aurelius, translated by Gregory Hays --- Discover how to ground yourself so you can understand that we are still the same despite our differences through time and space.

15. *Unshakeable: Your Financial Freedom Playbook* - Tony Robbins, Peter Mallouk --- Learn fundamental strategies for investing and its compound effects.

QUICK REFERENCES

Below you will find a list of organizations to reach out to based on your circumstances and needs. Have this list handy and make sure it can be easily accessed.

Organization Name	Phone Number	Web Address	What For?
Emergencies			
National Emergency Number	911		Emergencies and life threatening situations.
National Domestic Violence Hotline	1.800.799.7233		Get help with domestic violence.
National Sexual Assault Hotline	1.800.656.4673		Receive help with sexual assault cases.
National Human Trafficking Hotline	1.888.373.7888		Victims and survivors of human trafficking.
National Suicide Prevention Lifeline	1.800.273.8255		Suicide prevention network.

Immigration			
USCIS Case Status Check		*egov.uscis.gov/ casestatus*	Check USCIS case status, and find out processing times.
USCIS Filing Fees		*www.uscis. gov/fees*	Check current filing fees with USCIS.
USA Learns		*www. usalearns.org*	Learn English for free, get help with preparing for U.S. Citizenship test/ interview, learn job-related skills and about living in the States.
Personal Services			
Non-Emergency Number	311		A citizens' hotline that people can call in many cities to find information about services, make complaints, or report problems like graffiti or road damage.

Essential Community Services	211	*www.211.org*	Info on services for, among others, the elderly, the disabled, those who do not speak English, those with a personal crisis, those with limited reading skills, and those who are new to their communities.
Motor Vehicle Services		*www.usa.gov/ motor-vehicle-services*	Get driver's license and other vehicle related information.
United States Postal Service (USPS) Change of Address		*www.usps. com/umove*	Notify the United States Postal Service (USPS) to start forwarding your mail to your new address when you move.
Selective Service System		*www.sss.gov*	Register for Selective Service (required for all male citizens and immigrants aged 18-25)
StopBullying.gov		*www.stop bullying.gov*	Learn how to address and/ or report cases of bullying, including cyberbullying

Personal Finances			
Financial Literacy and Education Commission		*www. mymoney.gov*	Receive education about personal finance and money management.
Central Source LLC		*www. annualc reditreport.com*	Get one free copy of your credit report per year.
Assistance			
Benefit Finder		*www. benefits.gov*	Find out which benefit programs you may be eligible for and how to apply.
Federal Student Aid		*www. studentaid.gov*	Apply for financial aid through the Federal Student Aid program.

If you require legal help but don't have enough money to hire an attorney, try some of the following low-cost or free assistance options.

Immigration Law		
American Immigration Lawyers Association (AILA)	*www.aila.org*	An organization of more than 15,000 attorneys who teach and practice immigration law that represent international students, athletes, entertainers, and asylum seekers, often for free

National Immigration Legal Services Directory	*www. immigrationadvocates. org/legaldirectory*	Directory of nonprofit organizations that offer free or low-cost immigration legal services.
Executive Office for Immigration Review (EOIR) Accredited Organizations and Representatives	*www.bit. ly/3NjlwvU*	A directory of recognized organizations and accredited representatives arranged by that particular state/territory
Executive Office for Immigration Review (EOIR) Recognized Pro-Bono Attorneys and Organizations	*www.bit. ly/3ldDBPS*	A directory of attorneys and organizations that have agreed to help immigrants pro bono (free of charge) with immigration proceedings.
National Immigration Project of the National Lawyers Guild (NIPNLG)	*www.nipnlg.org*	An organization of lawyers and legal workers to defend and extend the rights of all noncitizens in the States.
Legal (Non-Immigration)		
U.S. Government Services and Information	*www.usa.gov/ legal-aid*	A list of free or low-cost legal assistance and resources recognized by USA.gov
Legal Services Corporation (LSC)	*www.lsc.gov*	A nonprofit organization that provides grants for civil legal assistance to low-income Americans.

LawHelp	*www.lawhelp.org*	An organization that helps people of low and moderate incomes find free legal aid programs in their communities, answers to questions about their legal rights and forms to help them with their legal problems

If you have an inquiry but are not sure which department can help you call 1.844-USAGOV1 (1.844.872.4681) or visit www.usa.gov.

List of Federal Departments & Agencies		
U.S. Department of Education (ED)	1.800.872.5327	*www.ed.gov*
U.S. Equal Employment Opportunity Commission (EEOC)	1.800.669.4000	*www.eeoc.gov*
U.S. Department of Health & Human Services (HHS)	1.877.696.6775	*www.hhs.gov*
U.S. Department of Homeland Security (DHS)	1.202.282.8000	*www.dhs.gov*
U.S. Citizenship & Immigration Services (USCIS)	1.800.375.5283	*www.uscis.gov*
U.S. Customs & Border Protection (CBP)	1.877.227.5511	*www.cbp.gov*
U.S. Immigration & Customs Enforcement (ICE)	1.866.347.2423	*www.ice.gov*
U.S. Department of Housing & Urban Development	1.202.708.1112	*www.hud.gov*
U.S. Department of Justice (DOJ)	1.202.514.2000	*www.justice.gov*

U.S. Department of the Treasury	1.800.829.1040	*www.treasury.gov*
Selective Service System (SSS)	1.847.688.6888	*www.sss.gov*
Social Security Administration (SSA)	1.800.772.1213	*www.social security.gov*
U.S. Department of State (DOS)	1.888.407.4747	*www.state.gov*

My fellow immigrants,

Thank you for joining me on this journey through this book. I hope the knowledge and insights I've shared will aid your adaptation and success as immigrants in the U.S.

Since the world is constantly evolving and information can transform in the blink of an eye, I encourage you to visit my website, www.ansimpact.com, so that you can stay up-to-date with relevant information and the latest developments. There, you'll also find a wealth of resources tailored to immigrants like us, providing updated insights and practical tips for your journey.

I stand beside you, cheering you on and believing in your incredible potential. Best of luck as you flourish in this beautiful land we now call home.

Best Regards,
Jon

Made in the USA
Middletown, DE
04 February 2024

48546166R00137